LEAD FROM WITHIN

MASTERING AUTHENTIC LEADERSHIP TO INSPIRE AND ACHIEVE

ADAM LEE

Lead From Within

Edited By: Kim Mary

Published by Lighthouse Reads

Printed in the United States of America

First Printing Edition, 2024

I S B N 979-8-330-41736-0

To Mom and Dad

Table of Contents

Preface

A sergeant in the United States Army is known for sharp discipline. His uniform must remain immaculate, his coyote brown boots always clean, and his face clean-shaven like a barren desert. To him, a soldier's appearance reflected their pride, professionalism, and commitment. He had little patience for those who fell short of the standard. His soldiers were aware of this—except for one.

Before sunrise, the sergeant awoke earlier than his squad. He conducted his morning routine, brushing his teeth, shaving his face, slipping on his morning physical training uniform, and heading to the standard formation area. Every morning, at the same time and place, his company would create an accountability formation, review last-minute details for the day, and, in unison, salute the American flag as reveille played. This was every soldier's routine before starting the day with physical training.

He had one soldier in particular who was quieter and more reserved and often seemed to lag in the small, seemingly insignificant details. Moments prior to formation, this private arrived with a patchwork of nicks and cuts, small amounts of blood seeping through the lacerations in his skin.

"What in God's name is this?" says the sergeant as he gestured to the mess on his soldier's face. "Do you think this is acceptable?"

"Sergeant, I… I tried my best." the private replies hesitantly.

"Clearly, your best isn't good enough," he snapped, frustration building. "Every soldier here manages to arrive clean-shaven every morning without looking like they've gotten into a knife fight. So, what's your problem?"

There was a silence that stretched too long. The sergeant snapped again, "Speak up, private!"

"I didn't have anyone to t—no one taught me how to shave, sergeant," mutters the private, his voice barely over a whisper. He swallows hard as his gaze drops to the ground.

The sergeant blinked. The words hung in the air, cutting through the sergeant's anger. He had remembered the private had grown up without his father. The soldier wasn't being lazy or careless. He wasn't failing out of neglect. He hadn't been taught.

The sergeant told his soldier to fall into formation and continued with the morning as if the interaction hadn't occurred. The sergeant then realized a life-changing realization: It was not the time to become frustrated or upset; it was time to lead.

From that morning onward, that sergeant shaved with his soldier for about a week until he had it down. He taught him how to lather, gave some tips for using warm water, and reminded him that the razor would work with light pressure and the proper angle. After Private Hackjob grew more confident and the cuts became fewer, his skin began to smooth out, and the awkward cuts and patches were traded for a clean, even shave.

"You did good." the sergeant said, nodding in approval. "That's how it should look. Well done."

Standing taller than before, the soldier nodded, quietly replying, "Thank you, S'rgnt."

As the sergeant walked away, he reflected on the week. The situation started with frustration—an instant explosion due to a lack of patience. The soldier didn't know how to shave because no one taught him. The sergeant realized leadership wasn't about barking orders and expecting results. Often, leadership is about stepping down from the pedestal of authority and meeting your followers where they are. It is about guidance and growth.

In that small act, that sergeant learned that leaders must identify a problem and choose to do something about it.

That sergeant was me. I was the naive leader who expected the world from someone unprepared to give it.

It was a lesson I'd wished I had known earlier but would not soon forget. For this reason, I've decided to compile a book outlining the various nuances and principles regarding the theory of leadership.

Leadership is a crucial force shaping our world, yet it is often misunderstood. Our ability to lead determines success in business, politics, education, and personal lives. Leadership is a theory, an invisible concept that connects our vision to action, ideas to results, and challenges people to achieve their highest potential. But what is leadership really? Is leadership the ability to command a team, give orders, inspire a crowd, or outthink competitors? The truth is that leadership is all these things and more. Leadership is about influence, integrity, and the ability to guide others. In modern terms, leadership brings out the best in people and empowers even the lowest on the totem pole.

Empowerment of the individual wasn't always the ordinary course. Leadership theory has evolved, shifting throughout millennia. This book serves to deliver valuable insight into leadership. We will discuss concepts and perspectives, with formidable action steps, that will enhance your leadership development and establish a growth mindset for you and those around you. I applaud your curiosity and understanding of why this idea is crucial and how you can develop the skills to lead effectively, regardless of your background or position. We'll explore timeless principles of leadership, uncover strategies that stand the test of time, and understand the new ways of empowerment. This book aims to provide a practical understanding of leaders' problems and offer ways to overcome them.

As I have, you'll learn that leadership isn't about perfection, innate talent, or a lucky start but more about growth, learning, and the willingness to act. In the chapters ahead, we will break down essential qualities that help make a leader and provide fresh perspectives you can use daily. Discover the practical tools you can use to build these traits for yourself and your team.

Most importantly, you'll understand that leadership is not a destination but a journey. It is a continuous process of learning, reflection, improvement, and inspiration. Whether you are the CEO, a small business owner, or fresh to the workforce, you'll better understand your potential to be a leader within your own right.

Since adopting the lessons outlined in this book, my life has had some radical changes. Since gaining a better understanding of myself, others, human behavior, and how to lead them all, I have been offered a better career field, earned multiple raises, thus earning more money, saved and, in turn, invested more money, lead more prominent teams, managed larger projects, improved my professional relationships, improved my relationships, managed my time more efficiently, pursued more personal interests, lowered my stress, enhanced my focus and concentration, become increasingly more confident in myself, understood how to delegate more efficiently, adapted better to last minute changes, learned how to invest in myself, and, arguably most importantly, learned how to cherish myself. While this list may not be all-encompassing, and perhaps you've already found the key to success, this book suggests that leadership is more than a title or position but a mindset. Our nature as humans is to be curious, wonder, and daydream. These wonders often make their way to the storybooks, and for those that work, they stick. This book offers a tried-and-true methodology of leadership philosophy that will enhance a surprisingly wide variety of aspects of your life. I want to take this moment to honor, validate, and appreciate your strides to better yourself and the world around you.

The need for inclusive leadership is becoming increasingly important in today's world. Effective leadership is not just about authority but also a venture into humility, which is the basis of our journey together.

This guide explores the significance of accountability and collaboration and how they contribute to inclusive leadership. Real-world examples will help us understand how this approach fosters diversity, equity, and inclusion within organizations and shapes the trajectory of influential, inclusive leaders.

Together, let's analyze what authentic leadership entails and pave the way for a future where our actions resonate with inclusivity. Let's learn how to lead within our organization; let's learn to lead within ourselves.

Chapter 1

WHAT LEADERS DO

Leaders play a crucial role in guiding, inspiring, and influencing others. Leaders possess a unique combination of vision, charisma, and strategic thinking, enabling them to navigate complex situations, inspire confidence, and foster collaboration. They not only point the direction but also set the pace through exemplary leadership. Through integrity, empathy, and resilience, leaders can confidently rise to any challenge and face it head-on. Whether you are already in a leadership position and looking to pass on some good qualities to your team leads or yearning for more responsibility and meaningful challenges, this book will equip you with the tools to become an effective and transformative leader. This chapter discusses the techniques and strategies for incorporating core beliefs, rules of conduct, authenticity, and developing resilience.

To produce effective leaders, we need to understand their roles. Leaders are visionaries, decision-makers, communicators, mentors, and role models. As we see, several factors define aspects of leadership. We will break down these different aspects as we continue, allowing for self-reflection and growth. There is a wide variety of leadership styles, but some core functions are essential for a great leader. Leaders establish a clear direction, purpose, and motivation for their team by creating a compelling vision. Communication soon follows suit, providing clarity in the vision and defining expectations.

A leader should clearly define the position of the team, the desired destination, and outline the steps to reach that destination. It is important for a leader to inspire purpose and a collective commitment to achieve business goals and objectives.

In addition, it is important to understand the strengths and personalities of your team members and ensure your vision aligns with their core beliefs. Setting measurable goals is vital for guiding your team and tracking their progress. When creating goals for your team, the results should be feasible and measurable. Communicating regularly with your team will enhance these processes during their development.

A person's character is built by their capacity to make good decisions related to personal or interpersonal relationships. A man's ethical and moral nature can be determined by their interpersonal relationships; the sum of an individual's views, values, attitudes, behaviors, and personal drive represents their character. "Good character" does not refer to a singular collection of characteristics. Instead, let's look at the factors that indicate a leader.

Beliefs and Principles of Conduct

Values and beliefs are the foundation of an individual's character. These beliefs are often deeply rooted in one's identity. One's values determine the importance attached to life choices and helps in making sound judgements.

Someone who has experienced poverty or starvation will most likely prioritize his/her self-preservation over political acceptance. Similarly, a boy who was once subject to rejection from his crush may hesitate to make a move on his next date. Humans are predisposed to conduct themselves based on a series of past experiences. Our minds consistently attempt to predict life's next move based on previous experiences. Every time we do something, we gain more experience.

It can be challenging to change an individual's values and beliefs, which are shaped by life experiences. Instead, as the mentor, you are responsible for explaining core principles and why it is important to promote them.

People value diverse things. It could be family, friendship, health, education, a successful career, financial security, creativity, freedom, nature, and community. However, this list is not all-encompassing and varies depending on cultural backgrounds, beliefs, and experiences.

As a leader, take time to understand those around you. Personally engage with your team, study their passions and drives, and learn who they are beyond their job description. By showing interest, you prove that you value your team members. This can help build trust and faith while providing vital information about how your team operates under pressure, how well they work with others, the accommodation they may require, etc.

Authenticity

One expression I frequently see as a pointer to integrity is "doing the right thing when nobody's watching." Consistency is attributed to someone's integrity. One-time honesty doesn't give someone integrity, as attending a gym session doesn't make someone an athlete. Integrity requires active and consistent action that matches words or professed values and is backed by authenticity. While conversations between peers and subordinates must remain professional, it's essential to acknowledge that we are sentient beings with thoughts, ideas, and curiosities. Do not be afraid to speak from the heart –just keep it professional.

Establishing a core set of moral principles and strictly adhering to them builds a habit of authenticity. Through authenticity, trust is fostered within the team, and unity is strengthened. Following these ethical principles and expressing standards of behavior fosters a positive reputation for the leader and strengthens relationships with the team. This translates to leaders taking accountability for their team's actions and their own.

To be an effective leader, support consistent honesty and use your influence to promote integrity. Consistency is an inherently tricky trait to obtain and takes lots of practice. Dogs are regarded as man's best friend, probably due to their consistency in expressing emotions and behavioral habits. Many of us love dogs solely because of their predictability. We know they will be excited to see us when we open the door. Establish the inherent importance of being dependable and trustworthy in your organization.

Moral Courage

A person's true nature becomes evident by their willingness to defend what is right. When confronted with challenges, the strength of this courage is brought to the forefront. Moral courage is the ability to address injustice, especially in the face of opposition and criticism. This kind of courage is grounded in authenticity, integrity, and responsibility, which leaders are expected to embody. The difficulty of displaying moral courage arises when leaders must confront their fears, overcome obstacles, and face the unknown. Nevertheless, moral courage is essential for successful leaders to experience personal growth and implement ethical decisions or policies.

Moral courage can be displayed in surprising ways. After noticing the malfunction of an assault craft boat on the Ong Muong Canal in South Vietnam, Lieutenant Thomas G. Kelley maneuvered his boat to act as a shield for the disabled troops. As the Vietnam War raged on, Kelley's boat was violently stuck by Viet Cong forces as they opened fire. Soon after the ambush commenced, a rocket-propelled grenade struck Kelley's boat, spraying shrapnel in all directions. This blast severely wounded the young lieutenant. While disregarding his injuries, Kelley continued to direct his ships and lead his men to safety. This gallantry earned him the Medal of Honor; Kelley stated, "Moral courage – doing what has to be done because it is the right thing to do."

The leader's habits will always be passed on to their followers, whether for the better or the worse. In addition to encouraging more productive employees, there are a few methods by which a leader might motivate individuals to give their best.

Vision

Leaders can develop the ideal team by creating a compelling vision of the future. An important consideration for every new leader is to familiarize themselves with the organization's goal. From here, leaders must formulate a strategy for how they and their team can improve these goals. The purpose of this should not necessarily be to say that the organization, business, or enterprise requires assistance; instead, the team's approach should complement the organization's objectives.

Improvements or recommendations should be carried out in a manner that indicates responsibility and a willingness to take the initiative. Visions can comprise a wide variety of traits; nonetheless, they should include a minimum of the following: an inspiring mental image, deeply connected ideals, and resilience. An influential leader can leave a lasting legacy for the team or unit by considering the three aspects listed above in their vision.

Creating a mental image to motivate others is a straightforward process that can be surprisingly successful. Leaders can recognize problems, worries, and legitimate complaints regarding their organization by listening to their subordinates. In many cases, particularly in huge businesses, the experience or opinions of subordinates are not considered essential, which can be detrimental to the organization.

Remember, your team is the "boots on the ground," physically carrying out the assigned tasks. They best understand the intricacies of the tasks. It is recommended that a meeting be organized to gather input, during which all members in specific roles are allowed to voice their concerns. Although sorting through these concerns may be tiresome, it will bring your followers' challenges to light. Understanding your subordinates' perspective enables them to picture the vision, ultimately ensuring its success. Create an image that satisfies all your requirements, then work backward. Setting expectations and opening effective lines of communication is crucial to a vision's development. After delivering his historic Gettysburg Address on November 19, 1863, Abraham

Lincoln finished his speech by painting a clear image for those listening. As the American Civil War continued its bloody conflicts in droves, Lincoln reminded his citizens:

"It is instead for us to be here dedicated to the excellent task remaining before us, that from these honored dead we take increased devotion to that cause for which they gave the last full measure of faith, that we here highly resolve that these dead shall not have died in vain, that this nation, under God, shall have a new birth of freedom, and that government of the people, by the people, for the people, shall not perish from the earth."

(Abraham Lincoln, 1863)

The original purpose of this address was to pay tribute to the approximately seven thousand men who lost their lives during the battle of Gettysburg, which took place from June 1st to 3rd, 1863. These men included both Union and Confederate soldiers. It is important to note that the latter half of his speech does not directly pertain to the conflict but speaks more about the people.

Although this speech is brief, it gives the audience various strategic insights. This is neatly wrapped up with a patriotic reminder that the government is there for the people it serves. Lincoln painted a clear image for others to follow, and they followed his example. One could argue that this speech inspired the Union troops to reorganize and mobilize with a fresh perspective.

Abraham Lincoln was a leader. He created clear mental images for subordinates, and he ultimately beat the Confederate army in April 1865. Although Lincoln has several different viewpoints, some cannot be disregarded. Under no circumstances should we undervalue the impact that an image of inspiration may have on other people; it could very well be the reminder they were looking for.

Implementing ideas related to your vision will leave a long-lasting legacy. Cross-cultural influence is better than it has ever been, and it is something leaders ought to take into consideration when they are formulating their vision. These values should not always be based on their personal convictions; they should be those the organization (and its people) can thrive on. Find out who the other people in your department are. Religious beliefs, cultural norms, customs, and patterns of behavior contribute to the formation of the values that your vision intends to develop.

One way to think about values is as a collection of guiding principles that influence other people's actions. These principles are often neglected or not openly expressed, leaving ethical boundaries vulnerable and expectations open to the individual's interpretation. Instead, you should ensure that your vision is built on a foundation that encourages alignment, ethical decision-making, trust, and inclusivity.

A mutual agreement encourages long-term sustainability and team success and attracts like-minded individuals with the same values. While clearly defining your value system clearly is essential, there should be room for innovation and flexibility. Principles should align with evolving perspectives.

Overcoming Obstacles

Lastly, every vision ought to be geared toward overcoming obstacles. Having a vision might not be essential if there is a rare chance to improve one specific part of your business. Essentially, having a vision means conquering particular challenges. In the highly odd event, if one single aspect of your business could be enhanced, then it is not necessary to have a vision. On a fundamental level, having a vision is synonymous with overcoming some challenges. During any trip, and especially in the role of a leader, one will inevitably encounter obstacles. If you take this course of action, you and your team can inculcate resiliency and tenacity while boosting confidence. Rather than viewing challenges as impediments to progress, encourage your team to view them as chances for growth that can enable them to overcome more effectively conquer the unknown.

Additionally, identifying specific obstacles to overcome helps the team be more committed, promotes teamwork, and discourages complacency. When selecting a challenge to overcome, it is essential to ensure that it is not just demanding but also attainable. In this scenario, it would not be appropriate (or supported) to use phrases like "ruling the world" or "no sick days this quarter."

Consider concepts that are more in line with historical records and the current protocol. For example, try to increase the amount of water you consume today compared to the previous day. Similarly, you may push your team to fulfill the project deadline one day earlier than last year or reduce the number of injuries that occur in the workplace this year. These are straightforward obstacles that directly challenge a team to try harder. Present more difficult challenges once you witness their confidence built by overcoming obstacles.

Rather than being the result of a sudden realization, visions are instruments purposefully and systematically crafted by leaders to express expectations effectively. A common baseline must be laid for followers to form their starting point. Using visions, which might range from short-term projects to long-term objectives, can help your team move forward and track their progress. Visions are things that leaders will utilize to explain their current situation and how they plan to accomplish their goals. Visions should be carefully considered, and they must be communicated sincerely. It is inappropriate to utilize visions to condemn others for their wrongdoings or to take disciplinary action against them. Both leaders and visions must continue to be accurate, and leaders must continue to have faith in their visions.

Develop an authentic vision that promotes moral courage and motivates others to overcome obstacles.

Chapter 2

DIFFERENT STYLES OF LEADERSHIP

Leadership is a multifaceted concept that incorporates several styles and approaches. Leaders give directives and inspire others to follow them, establish unity, and ensure team success. Because there is only a general approach to leadership, studying different styles and ways to become a more unique and impactful leader is helpful.

From authoritative to laissez-faire leadership styles, leadership theories offer various strategies to guide and inspire leaders. Those in leadership roles need to understand and harness the nuances of leadership. This chapter discusses the intricacies of leadership styles, their perspectives, and applications. Effective leadership does not emerge through adopting a specific style, but a combination of diverse approaches rooted in authenticity, ethics, understanding, and commitment to positive change.

The most popular leadership styles are authoritarian, democratic, and laissez-faire. Autocratic leaders typically believe subordinates are inherently lazy, requiring constant direction and control. This attitude makes followers less likely to take initiative without orders. This was the approach I implemented when I was first placed in charge of others. I foolishly assumed this role. My persona took on a high-stress, low-risk attitude, concluding that no subordinate under my watch could make the proper decision independently. My authoritarian approach did not help develop those under my umbrella into critical-thinking, confident leaders. Under the authoritarian approach, leaders focus on announcing the organization's goal, directing their team, and encouraging them to invest their efforts in realizing it. It is important to note that while these leaders can come down with a heavy hammer, they are *effective.* Authoritarian leaders can accomplish this by identifying goals and inspiring the confidence of their team so they can overcome obstacles and build success.

On the opposite end of the spectrum lies laissez-faire, also known as delegation leadership. Laissez-faire leaders delegate decisions to their team and provide guidance, but ultimately trust they will take responsibility and accomplish tasks independently. If you've been in the workforce for some time, you've encountered this type of leader. Unfortunately, this type of management is not often seen in senior and high-ranking positions. The laissez-faire-esque approach is typically seen as too calm and unstructured. Like the authoritative approach, laissez-faire can work. However, this is seen mainly with leaders who lack the confidence to achieve the mission and thus rely on subordinates to (hopefully) take care of business.

Next is the middle ground – the democratic leader. He emphasizes the importance of collaboration and inclusiveness. Leaders of a democratic nature prefer involving their team members in decision-making processes, creating a feeling of ownership and mutual responsibility. These leaders translate their group's collective wisdom and creativity into solutions. This style makes brainstorming easier, especially when faced with complex problems. Instead of ruling with an iron fist, democratic leaders facilitate the development process and offer guidance and inspiration to their followers, increasing their likelihood to initiate movement and encapsulate responsibility. These leaders also consider some form of self-reflection to identify personal shortcomings and possible solutions. Democratic leaders value the process as much as the results.

Since each approach has inherent benefits, it can be easily applied to different situations. The team's specific needs will dictate how it is applied. The secret of being a good leader is being aware of the specialties and weaknesses of all the styles and adapting accordingly.

While the emergence of various leadership styles suggests that each approach has strengths and weaknesses, some styles better suit some situations. Now, let us examine each one closely, analyze its strengths and weaknesses, and determine how it should be applied.

Authoritative Leadership:

Advantages:

- Provides clear direction: Authoritarian leaders are known for efficiently defining a strategy and communicating organizational values and goals. Therefore, there is strict adherence to the team's objective.
- Fosters efficiency: This leadership style is known for timely decision-making, which can save time and keep projects on track by reducing redundancy.
- Excels in crises: Authoritarian leaders excel in stressful circumstances because their quick decision-making capabilities allow them to take decisive action and offer direction when necessary. This style is often seen in high-stress environments such as military, law enforcement, emergency services, etc.
- Inspires confidence: Authoritative leaders build the trust of team members by displaying mastery and decisiveness, which increases motivation and productivity.

Disadvantages:

- Can stifle creativity: The necessity of a clear direction and following the existing procedures may reduce the chances for innovation and creative problem-solving.
- May limit engagement: Authoritarian leadership may sometimes stifle communication and neglect the involvement of others, which may lead to reduced engagement or commitment due to a lack of individual ownership.

Best Used When:

- An urgent deadline or a time-sensitive project needs decision-making and action on the spot.
- A clear direction should be pursued, especially in contexts where following existing protocols is of the utmost importance, such as heavily regulated sectors.

Laissez-Faire Leadership:

Advantages:

- Empowers employees: Laissez-faire leaders delegate tasks to team members so everyone becomes accountable and capable of making decisions.
- Encourages ownership and initiative: This leadership style creates an atmosphere of self-determination, allowing employees to be proactive and creative and develop their problem-solving skills.
- Fosters innovation: Laissez-faire leadership enables team members to develop new ideas and determine the best approaches, leading to higher levels of innovation and productivity among the group.

Disadvantages:

- Can lead to confusion or lack of direction: Some team members might not understand their roles and assignments, which can lead to disorientation or an inability to follow instructions.
- Not suitable for inexperienced teams or those requiring close supervision: Laissez-faire leadership is for experts and people who need little attention to work productively. Sometimes, the highly independent, directive leadership pattern may be a barrier to the junior team members or those needing close supervision. This approach will crumble a team that is not inherently self-motivated.

Best Used When:

- Working with highly skilled, self-motivated individuals who thrive on autonomy and responsibility.
- Fostering innovation and creativity, as this leadership style allows individuals to explore new ideas and approaches.
- Delegating well-defined tasks to individuals capable of taking ownership and making decisions.

Democratic Leadership:

Advantages:

- Boosts morale: Giving team members a chance to participate in decision-making will help them feel appreciated and respected, resulting in high morale and great satisfaction. Democratic leaders still need to maintain control of the decision-making process.
- Fosters innovation: A democratic leadership style that promotes inclusiveness and diversity of thought has many benefits, such as igniting creativity and innovation among team members.
- Leads to well-rounded decisions: Democratic leaders can make prompt and well-rounded decisions through discussion and gathering views from the right team members. Experience and personal confidence play a vital role during this process.

Disadvantages:

- Can be time-consuming: Democratic leadership often has a collaborative component, which involves consulting different people. This can be time-consuming and impractical in dynamic situations. To negate this, establish reasonable timeframes for collaboration.

- May not be ideal for large groups: The goal is often farther when working with large teams, making it more challenging to integrate every team member's idea and preference. Allow junior leaders to represent sections of the team and encourage them to communicate with their team members actively.

Best Used When:

- Brainstorming solutions or generating ideas, as the democratic approach encourages diverse perspectives and fosters a sense of ownership among team members.
- Building team spirit and promoting a positive work environment. Involving team members in decision-making enhances their sense of belonging and investment in the team's success.
- Tackling complex problems that require different viewpoints and expertise, as democratic leadership can help leverage the collective wisdom and creativity of the team.

Knowledge of different leadership styles can make leaders more flexible and efficient. Every style has merits and demerits, and their application is based on the situation at hand, the team's needs, and the actual outcomes. A leader who is conscious of these styles and their impact can adapt their strategies to motivate, facilitate teamwork, and direct in the best interest of their teams.

Let's be honest: most of the leadership styles we learn about in books seem like abstract ideas. Authoritarian, democratic, laissez-faire—all these sound like good options, but bringing them to life is another thing altogether. As for me, the road to realizing effective leadership is quite rough (full of ups and downs).

When I first stepped into a leadership role, I naively assumed people needed constant direction and control. I became this high-strung leader, obsessed with getting the "right" answer and minimizing risks. As a young soldier in the United States Army, I was informed of the three golden nuggets necessary to be a good soldier: the right place, time, and uniform. This seemed simple enough, and after a few years of showing up on time and following through with my tasks, I was considered for a leadership position. While it may be some time before my official promotion, I oversaw four other soldiers, some older than me. Having only the experience of my previous leader's approach, I took charge the only way I knew how. It was all about the results—measurable outcomes and finished products. Looking back, I realize I completely missed the point. The process of learning and growing as a team is just as, if not more, important than the final product.

My focus on control stifled any chance of developing my team into critical thinkers and confident leaders. Sure, I could have gone entirely hands-off, laissez-faire style, but that wouldn't have fostered any actual development. I needed a middle ground.

The solution was to be a democratic leader. I needed to change my approach. I thought back to a book my father gave me on my 15th birthday – *How to Win Friends and Influence People* by Dale Carnegie. What a great insight into communication and perspective that was. Instead of giving orders, I tried to keep them moving by using ideas such as suggestions and motivations. I wanted them to be able to own the characters, make decisions, and learn from their mistakes.

I needed the reminder that there is no one way to skin a cat. At the end of the day, we are all humans with unique thoughts, feelings, stressors, dreams, and emotions. That realization inspired me to write this book.

It was a real eye-opener. Self-reflection helped me assess my leadership style, evaluate my flaws, and move towards a better approach. The change to a more democratic model was as dramatic a transformation as night is from day. In the end, my team became more engaged, more collaborative, and much more enjoyable to work with. We weren't just hammering out outcomes but studying and training ourselves as a team.

This experience taught me a valuable lesson: Leadership is not about knowing everything or being the boss of others. It is about building an atmosphere where everyone feels confident enough to give their best effort. It is about creating a team culture of mutual respect, learning, and shared values. This is the best part of being a leader for me. While positive results are naturally rewarding, the real reward is witnessing the continuous development of your team. Consider this during your team's next project.

Leadership does not have a "one size fits all solution." The finest leader possesses the know-how of different styles, such as those listed in this chapter. They can change their approach according to the circumstance, team make-up, and desired outcome.

Becoming a great leader is also about discovering oneself. Leadership begins with a simple trial-and-error process that teaches everything from creating an ideal environment that favors teamwork to empowering individuals and building a collaborative vision. It's not just about winning but about understanding the process of working as a team toward success.

Appreciate the agony and joy that comes with the journey. Remember, leadership is not about controlling others. It is about creating environments where people have the opportunity to show their best qualities.

Chapter 3

TRAITS OF SUCCESSFUL LEADERS

Leaders are inherently in a unique position. While they are expected to give instructions, decipher and disseminate information, and direct teams to accomplish the mission, they also provide opportunities for growth and track the progress of their subordinates. A leader must identify frictions and wholeheartedly resolve them. Even through the face of challenge lies the reward of overcoming obstacles. Before discussing the traits of well-known leaders, let's discuss the importance of building interpersonal relationships.

Ask yourself what you've done today. Ask yourself if you are challenging your abilities in a way that would make you proud of yourself. Are you proud of yourself? While we are usually aware of what we want, what steps have you taken to accomplish what you *need* to accomplish? Have you done the hard thing lately? Have you stopped to consider the leaders in your life and adequately appreciate their guidance and support? Endeavor to use your time wisely and effectively, as your followers are always watching.

As a leader, you will always be under the watchful gaze of your subordinates; your presence or absence will be noticed, your patience will be remembered, and those brief anecdotes will be taken to heart. While this book is not intended to provide parental advice, an excellent example of this idea lies within childhood – kids are always looking up to mom and dad for guidance, support, and structure.

The mind will usually quit way before the body does. Of course, challenging yourself physically through exercise has inherent and well-known benefits, but how often do we train the mind? The egocentric mind has an innate inability to differentiate between self and others. This restricts the mind from developing perspectives other than its own, often to its detriment. How frequently have you considered doing the difficult thing only to have the mind talk you out?

Often, the mind is made up even before facing adversity. Even after a good day with high energy, the mind will talk us out of going to the gym with excuses like, "You've worked hard enough today" or "You deserve a break." To understand the flaws in your leadership development, you must dig deep and confront the psyche that rejects change and prefers comfort. Only then can we identify and address our friction points. Reflect on yourself and take time to analyze your leadership.

As we review renowned leaders, I must first mention that being a leader is not a position. Leadership is a way of thinking, a school of thought, a philosophy, and a lifestyle. Effective leadership must be accomplished in three domains and in order. By doing so, we will recognize our abilities inward and branch out. The first domain is the personal domain.

This domain highlights the importance of leadership within oneself. It does not address others you plan to lead but asks a vital question: how are you leading yourself? It's essential to have mentors, teachers, coaches, and instructors to help reinforce your structural leadership and support this foundation. However, the leadership traits we must first heed are those within ourselves.

We must be confident that we will find a way to address any situation, even against insurmountable odds. Trust yourself to take initiative without the input of others. Embrace the idea that you are your own leader. The likelihood of achieving success, happiness, wealth, and freedom diminishes if you cannot embrace your personal leadership. To understand how to lead others, we must lead from within.

Once you've gained confidence in who you are, how you lead, and your ability to approach uncomfortable situations, you can move into the next domain, relational leadership. This domain relates to how you present yourself to those around you, specifically those you trust. This group could include friends, family members, your significant other, coaches, or a dependable supervisor. The relational domain consists of those closest to you.

Consider how your close friends view you. Are you regarded as reliable and consistent? Are you confident in yourself? Do the people you trust also trust your capabilities? Remember, leadership development is a process, not a product. These questions and considerations should be frequently reviewed.

The last domain is what I call the external domain. This domain delves into the idea of influencing others – particularly outsiders. These are individuals with whom an inherent trust has not been established. Moreover, there is often an innate distrust of the incoming leader. While experience will help make you a more outgoing and approachable leader, there will always be a sense of apprehension when entering a new group. Just as the past is not an accurate measure of the stock market, our previous interactions with new leaders, both good and bad, are what people will naturally revert to.

Unfortunately, this is the most imperative domain when reflecting on leadership development. This domain incorporates our work life and managerial duties. To best fulfill this aspect of governance, we must keep training until we've mastered our interpersonal stewardship and relational influence. The external domain of leadership is the area of leadership in which we are often most judged.

Great leaders inspire, motivate, and guide others toward a shared vision. But what are the peculiar attributes that distinguish them from others? This chapter will discuss some of the main traits of successful leaders and bring out the leader in you. Immerse yourself in the highlighted domains above; ask yourself if they apply to you and how to practice the teachings.

1. The Foundation: Integrity and Self-Awareness

At the core of effective leadership is integrity. This refers to honesty, including ethical principles and the ability to keep one's word. People believe leaders should be honest and trustworthy in discharging their duties. Think of integrity as the bedrock on which all other leadership qualities rest. Remember, your followers are watching.

Self-awareness builds on this foundation; leaders must know their strengths, weaknesses, values, and motivations. A self-aware leader can recognize bias, modify the communication style to different audiences, and use their strengths for the team's good. Self-awareness is a powerful self-assessment tool for maximizing leadership approach.

A leader with integrity gains the trust and respect of his team. People follow a leader they think is making fair decisions and acting ethically. Integrity requires self-awareness which enables leaders to know their biases and even blind spots; they will, therefore, be open to looking for varied perspectives that will lead to informed, rounded decisions.

2. Communication: Bridging the Gap

If integrity is the core of effective leadership, then communication is indeed the foremost edge. It involves clearly articulating your vision, ideas, and expectations. Indeed, this not only means that you talk but also actively listen. Your team members will not tell you everything you need to know if they aren't being challenged, motivated, praised, etc. Effective communication requires patience and insight on when (and how) to engage. Adaptable leaders can thus shift their conversation style to varied audiences to ensure that all are spoken to and feel understood. Imagine communication as a bridge that connects you and your team so that collaboration and shared purpose can flow back and forth.

Proper communication moves the message around so that every team member knows what objectives, expectations, and strategies are in place. This clarifies purpose and keeps everything moving in one direction. Leaders can adjust their communication to address personal needs and concerns through active listening. This tailored approach gets everyone involved and motivates them to do their best. Open communication should be clear, concise, and consistent.

3. Empathy: Walking in Another's Shoes

Great leaders are empathetic. They understand and feel for their team members. Empathy establishes trust that further builds a more positive work environment, empowering leaders to inspire individuals toward what is peculiar to their needs and dreams. Think of empathy as the key to unlocking your team's full potential. In other words, once the team's perspective is made aware, leaders can create a space where everyone feels valued and supported.

Knowledge of team members' aspirations and motivation enables a leader to effectively speak to their hearts and minds. Adopting individualized approaches engages individual strengths and leads to higher performance. Learn who your subordinates are.

4. Vision: Charting the Course

Leaders paint a picture of the future—a compelling vision that excites and motivates those who follow. Vision provides a clear direction and purpose; everybody knows why their work counts. Imagine vision as a lighthouse—it guides your team through challenges and keeps them focused on the ultimate goal.

A shared purpose represents a compelling vision through which the very sense of "why" one is doing what they do is meant to be given to every team member, making them more committed and dedicated. A clear vision is a roadmap that guides the team's strategy and decision-making processes. This ensures everyone is working towards the same goal via strategic direction.

5. Inspiring Action: Lighting a Fire

Great leaders don't talk the talk; they walk the walk. They inspire their team members to act, go the extra mile, and excel in delivery. It works through recognition, empowerment, and giving the individual opportunities for growth and development. Don't hesitate to praise others, particularly in front of their peers.

A leader's enthusiasm regarding their vision is infectious to followers. Such high spirits reinforce a positive working environment that motivates people to contribute positively. Team members' empowerment enables them to nourish independence in performance, leading to a high degree of self-driven performance and realizing potential growth. Development and growth are enabled through an enthusiastic culture of learning.

6. Resilience: Bouncing Back from Setbacks

The course of leadership is seldom smooth. A leader must run at odds, face challenges, and often fail. He must always learn to take it on the chin and bounce back. Resilient leaders bounce back from adversity, learn from mistakes, and move on confidently. Resilience can be easily pictured as the waves crashing into the beach. Day or night, rain or shine, the waves never rest. As everyone drifts into their slumber, the waves crash onto the shore without regard for previous attempts. That's resiliency.

Resilient leaders can recover from setbacks, learn from mistakes, and keep the team moving forward with a positive attitude. This inspires confidence and trust within the team, even during challenging times. Resilience allows leaders to adapt to unforeseen circumstances and solve problems creatively, which is of prime importance in the modern world, where everything is continuously changing.

7. Continuous Learning: A Growth Mindset

With the world being dynamic, leadership should be elastic. Successful leaders are lifelong learners; they offer new ideas, feedback, and ways of doing things. They have a growth mindset, meaning they believe their ability will improve with effort and perseverance. Think of a growth mindset as a compass—it keeps you adaptable to the shifting leadership landscape.

Keep in mind that leadership is not a goal but a journey. Developing these characteristics progressively paves the way to self-realization as a leader and assists others in reaching their potential. I remind my students to "do good things and never stop learning."

The world of leadership is constantly evolving. Leaders with a growth mindset will always look for ways to expand their skills and knowledge base. A growth mindset naturally evokes the acceptance of mistakes and challenges as opportunities to learn, readily forming a learning culture within the team. Effective leaders want to learn.

How Key Traits Foster Effective Leadership?

We have discussed a few essential elements of good leadership. Read on to see how those elements contribute to formulating a solid and effective leadership style.

You can do things differently by developing these qualities and incorporating them into your leadership style. After all, leadership is a journey, and one can always find more room for growth. Embrace the process, continuously learn and improve, and inspire your team to achieve great things.

Real-World Examples of Effective Leadership

The qualities we've discussed aren't just theoretical concepts – they're the building blocks of real-world leadership success. Let's examine some famous samples that illustrate how these traits manifest in action:

The Power of Integrity: Abraham Lincoln

Abraham Lincoln, the 16th President of the United States, is one of the leaders who exemplified integrity. He maintained honesty and fairness throughout his career, even against political gains. During the Civil War, influential politicians pressured him to suppress a critical newspaper. Lincoln famously replied, "You can't have a free country and have an unfree press." Such dedication to truth and justice, even if uncompromising to rigidity and bringing him quite a lot of trouble, still got him the utmost respect from the American nation and imbedded his name deep in history as one of the great leaders with moral fiber.

Communication for Success: Jacinda Ardern

New Zealand Prime Minister Jacinda Ardern is known for her clear, empathic communication style. In the aftermath of the 2019 mosque shootings in Christchurch, she gave a moving and powerful speech to the nation. She spoke directly to the Muslim community, expressing her sorrow and commitment to support them. Plain-word usage, genuine emotion, and a focus on shared values throughout the speech caused an intense response among New Zealanders and the world, pointing at the power of effective communication for unison and healing in crises.

Leading with Empathy: Satya Nadella

The CEO of Microsoft, Satya Nadella, is an active listener who makes team members feel included in the company's decision-making process. After concerns arose from soon-to-be parents, Nadella offered generous benefits for parental leave. This demonstrated empathy for the working parents. Such an empathetic approach lifted the employees' morale, enabling Microsoft to recruit and retain their organization's crème de la crème. Whether the approach was critically planned or strategic is irrelevant, as the lasting impression on its audience was acceptance and empathy.

The Power of Vision: Martin Luther King Jr.

Dr. Martin Luther King Jr. was a leader whose vision inspired change. His vision of America and society without racial prejudice inspired millions of Americans. His famous speech, "I Have a Dream," poeticized what America could and should be in the future and inspired a vibrant civil rights movement. By presenting an idealistic yet attainable vision, King was able to gain overwhelming support.

Inspiring Action: Nelson Mandela

Nelson Mandela, the former president of South Africa, is an inspiring leader. After 27 years of imprisonment, he emerged as a reconciling and forgiving leader. He took upon himself the togetherness of black and white South

Africans under one umbrella, inspiring the nation to advance in the vision of uniting the wounds from history's racial bitterness. His commitment to peace and firm belief in a better future ignited hope and inspired millions of people within and outside South Africa.

Resilience in Action: Winston Churchill

Against seemingly insurmountable odds, Churchill inspired the British people with unwavering determination and probably the best speeches ever given. One of the most famous lines from his "We Shall Fight on the Beaches" speech: "We shall fight on the beaches, we shall fight on the landing grounds, we shall fight in the fields and the streets, we shall fight in the hills; we shall never surrender," was not just a motivational quote from the British Prime Minister but a declaration of resilience against all odds.

Lifelong Learning: Indra Nooyi

Indra Nooyi, the outgoing CEO of PepsiCo, is the epitome of continuous learning. She was always on the watch for fresh information and opened her arms to new technologies to keep PepsiCo ahead of a rapidly developing market. She paved the way for healthier (looking) snack choices, knowing the soon-to-hit health-conscious wave of consumers. Ever the constant learner, this focus on lifelong learning continually empowered her to evolve strategies within PepsiCo to keep the company at the forefront of the food and beverage industry. She learned that consumers like to spend money on things marketed as "good for you," so she effectively made Pepsi products appear as such.

These are just a few examples of how leaders have developed the key traits we discussed to achieve remarkable success. By learning from their experiences and incorporating these principles into your leadership style, you can inspire and empower others to achieve great things. Let's examine a few more influential personalities and extract the principles mentioned earlier.

Abraham Lincoln: Integrity, Resilience, and Leadership

Lincoln's leadership during the Civil War exemplifies the power of these critical traits. His unwavering integrity was evident in his commitment to abolish slavery, even when faced with immense political pressure to compromise. This dedication to his principles earned him the trust and respect of many, both within the Union and abroad.

Resilience also played a crucial role in Lincoln's leadership. He faced numerous setbacks during the war, including military defeats and public dissent. However, he never wavered in his determination to preserve the Union. His resilience kept the country unified and focused on achieving victory.

Lincoln's leadership went beyond military strategy. He delivered powerful speeches that rallied the nation and articulated a clear vision for a united America. His Gettysburg Address is a testament to his ability to inspire hope and purpose even in the darkest times.

Marie Curie: Curiosity, Perseverance, and Scientific Innovation

Insatiable curiosity fueled Marie Curie's groundbreaking discoveries. She was constantly questioning the world around her, driven by a desire to understand the fundamental nature of matter. This curiosity led her to explore the world of radioactivity, a field still in its infancy.

Perseverance was essential for Curie's success. The research on radioactivity was arduous and dangerous. She faced numerous challenges, including limited resources, inadequate lab conditions, and skepticism from the scientific community. However, she persevered through these obstacles, driven by her passion for scientific discovery.

Curie's dedication to scientific innovation was groundbreaking. She developed new techniques for isolating radioactive elements and conducting radiation experiments and even coined the term radioactivity. Her innovative approach paved the way for advancements in nuclear physics and medicine.

Marcus Aurelius: A Stoic Leader

Marcus Aurelius exemplified stoic principles during his reign as emperor. His philosophical wisdom guided his leadership, emphasizing reason, self-control, and acceptance of that which lies beyond our control. This philosophy helped him navigate the challenges of war, illness, and political turmoil.

Marcus Aurelius' reign was characterized by firm determination. He remained resolute despite adversity, leading the Roman Empire with strength and resilience. His moral integrity ensured his commitment to justice and the well-being of his citizens, even during difficult times.

Wisdom in adversity is evident in Marcus Aurelius' writings, particularly "Meditations." These reflections reveal his ability to find inner peace and acceptance, even amidst external chaos. His stoic legacy inspires people today, offering guidance on navigating life's challenges with grace and resilience.

George Washington: Leading the Revolution and Building a Nation

George Washington's role in the American Revolution was a testament to his exceptional leadership. He instilled discipline and a sense of unity within the Continental Army, leading them to victory against the British. His strategic insight was crucial in planning key battles and securing the nation's independence.

Washington's commitment to virtue and integrity was legendary. He was a man of his word, earning the trust and respect of his fellow revolutionaries and foreign allies. This dedication to ethical leadership set a high standard for future American presidents.

Washington's humility and selflessness were evident in his willingness to relinquish power after two terms as President. This act solidified the principles of a democratic republic and demonstrated his commitment to the nation's best interests over personal ambition. Nation-building and unity were key goals of Washington's presidency. He worked tirelessly to establish a suitable federal government and promote economic growth. His leadership fostered a sense of national identity among the newly formed states, laying the foundation for a prosperous and united America.

By studying how these historical figures used vital leadership traits, we gain valuable insights into what makes a leader genuinely successful. Their legacies inspire us and serve as a roadmap for aspiring leaders.

Chapter 4

MENTORING AND COACHING

An organization's continued success and growth are determined by its ability to sustain itself organically. Companies can ensure longevity and promote internal resilience by empowering their members. If a leader leaves, the organization should be able to continue operations smoothly. Creating more leaders allows for better scalability, ensuring the team can continue performing without decreasing efficiency or effectiveness. In short, leaders create other leaders.

Leaders who fail to promote development from within will stifle productivity. Establishing a "my way or the highway" approach is a personality-based system that only operates efficiently when a specific leader is in charge. It does not allow flexibility or innovation. This chapter discusses communication with junior leaders and nurturing their development.

Mentoring and coaching are essential components to developing follow-on leadership. Regular training will contribute to your junior leader's professional development, engagement, organizational retention, and personal success. Let's examine the three essential areas where mentoring and coaching make a big difference:

1. Planning with Clear Objectives

Life in the army was busy – I was constantly preparing equipment, communicating with my team, and training for the unknown. I could find time during the evenings to attend college, but not nearly as often as I'd like. It wasn't until after my service that I could finally attend college full-time. I was ecstatic to focus much of my time on my studies. When my calculus class rolled around, I began to reconsider my excitement. However, I knew I'd never be able to conquer my shortcomings in math class if I embraced the idea that I would never be good enough.

Upon completing my math classes, I tutored high school-aged students in their math classes. Early on, I learned the parents needed to silence their inclination to make discouraging comments about their math skills. We've heard these before; "I was never good at math" or "Math was always my least favorite subject." While my students were overwhelmed by learning math, changing their perspective might offer reassurance.

Until about seventh grade, students learn the basics of arithmetic – the study of numbers and the operations between them. This is when students are exposed to addition, subtraction, multiplication, and division operations. However, these generally only work if we include an equal sign balancing both sides of the equation. Consider the following equation:

$$10 + 2 = 12$$

This makes complete sense, granted we understand the information on both sides of the equation. This is where I address my students' perspectives and help them tackle their fear of the unknown. Using this example, I ask what would happen if we did not know every part of the equation. Instead, we have an unknown component. We can label this unknown using the symbol 'y'. So now our new equation looks like this:

$$10 + y = 12$$

Common sense will tell us that 'y' is equivalent to the value of 2, but that's beside the point. This is the exact moment I would suggest a new perspective on math. We often know where we are and usually where we want to be. The stress comes from not knowing how to get there. But this is life – this is a much more realistic approach to navigating the complexities of existence. We can take steps in the right direction by starting with what we know (the lessons, laws, and rules from past experiences). Eventually, all students would conclude the answer is 2. Viola! I'd congratulate them on understanding the basic idea of Algebra.

The point of this story is not to tutor you in your math. Rather, this infers that even in math, we need a roadmap. Whether it's doing our homework or planning a cross-country road trip, we typically understand where to start and where we'd like to end up. The problem lies in the middle part – the unknown.

While mentoring future leaders, consider planning. Analyze where your mentees are now and where you'd expect them to be. Then, identify the unknown and discuss methods to reach the desired destination. This means establishing clear, attainable goals but constructing them in smaller, more digestible steps. These goals should fit with the team's overall goals and individual goals.

Let's consider the local restaurant's busser who aspires to one day step into management. A keen leader would help develop a plan to help his employees achieve this goal. We know where the busser is – setting tables, refilling drinks, and removing dirty dishes. We also know who the busser would like to become: a manager. To get there, let's suggest a series of small, attainable goals that would help him develop. Suggestions could include arriving at least five minutes before his shifts to ensure he does not clock in late, communicating a desire to help the waiting staff and learn more about what they do, and practicing his customer service skills by engaging in positive interactions with patrons. Although simple, this empowers the busser to take tangible steps towards more responsibility and further development as a leader.

This is how to see it: When your team members know where they're going and how their work fits into the bigger picture, they are more interested, focused, and, most of all, more successful.

2. How to Practice Active Listening

For a team to work well, everyone needs to be able to understand each other. But talking isn't enough. Mentoring and coaching require active listening. Pay close attention to what your environment is telling you. Maybe you've noticed your assistant manager shows up 10 minutes late to her shifts, often arriving stressed. Does she not care? Or could this indicate a problem with her schedule, vehicle, or previous obligations?

Your team will often tell you everything you need to know. Unfortunately, it is easy to forget to listen. Instead of waiting for our turn to speak, leaders must try to understand and appreciate the feedback they are given. Ask yourself if our example assistant manager is dissatisfied with her job. Consider if there is something you can do as a leader to help improve her work environment, ensure more consistent timeliness, and reduce stress. By opening lines of communication to understand the other party, we are priming ourselves to receive genuine feedback.

When you listen actively, you do far more than hear what someone is saying. You gain precious insight into all the nuances your team is facing.

Active listening only works if team members feel safe discussing their worries, thoughts, and goals. You can help build trust and psychological safety by making the workplace open and accepting. When your team feels they can speak freely, you will gain awareness of deficiencies and provide more specific help and advice. Adopting an active listening approach will reliably develop your leaders to become more patient, confident, and understanding when overcoming obstacles.

Think about this: When your team members feel like they are being understood, they are more likely to be open to new ideas, take small risks, and help solve problems. Everyone wants to be heard.

3. The Gift of Feedback:

Creating an environment of continuous learning requires the acceptance of feedback. Feedback provides valuable information on areas for improvement. Professional development and creative problem-solving both benefit from feedback. While not all feedback is positive, all feedback is important.

What allows feedback to become constructive is redirecting focus on specific actions, not traits. Communicate your team members' actions or behaviors that could use attention. Condemning feedback such as, "You're just bad at presentations," could be reframed as, "Let's look into how your presentations can increase audience engagement." Criticism should always be helpful and structured in a way that supports your team members. Leaders should not hesitate to encourage their team by providing them with the proper tools and training.

Equally important is to follow up on the feedback. Did you see any improvements in the next presentation? Communicate your observations and give a sincere "job well done!" You are, after all, their leader who is responsible for providing guidance and learning opportunities.

Remember that feedback should be beneficial. Instead of dwelling on mistakes, think about how your team can grow and reach its full potential. This will increase confidence to explore new problem-solving strategies. When you give your team members helpful feedback, they can better deal with problems, learn from their mistakes, and keep improving. This continuous growth makes the team more innovative, flexible, and effective.

Mentoring and coaching are not one-time events. Regular feedback helps team members communicate and build trust.

Building Your Team Strength:

Have you ever asked yourself, "Who in this team could become a leader someday?" The good news is that people often have leadership abilities just waiting to be discovered and developed. You have the power as a leader to give your team members the tools they need to reach their full potential. The question is how to find that secret skill and help it grow.

Here is how:

Lead by Example:

Leading by example is no simple feat. It requires consistent honesty, professionalism, and the continuous pursuit of improvement. As mentioned earlier in this book, leadership starts with the self. By becoming who you need to be, you are more likely to lead by example.

In other words, leaders must learn to do right by themselves before expecting others to follow suit. Actions speak louder than words; hence, you must be the model you want your followers to emulate. Never should a leader adopt a "check down, not up mindset." Also known as "do as I say, not as I do," this approach suggests that leaders are not required to set an example yet expect others to maintain the standard.

This inconsistency in words and actions is called cognitive dissonance. It occurs when behavioral decisions and attitude changes causes serious problems in both professional and personal settings. Leading by example acknowledges the nuances and pushes you to develop the habits you want your followers to embody.

In other words, you must show them the behaviors and traits you want them to have. You should be seen as honest, professional, and always looking for improvement. What you do says more than what you say. Repeating these traits will send a strong message to your team.

Encourage Growth Mindset

Every position we find ourselves in is a stepping stone. Review your interactions with strangers over the past week. Notice how seemingly content others become in their current positions. This is neither positive nor negative but simply an observation. These stepping stones often become permanent residences when people cannot expand their skills and knowledge base.

Encourage and reward creative thinking. Allow your team members to take charge of their skill growth. Motivating them to make choices, accept mistakes as learning opportunities, and lead themselves to achieve their goals. Believe in your team member's ability to grow.

Getting ahead isn't always easy. Things will go wrong, and problems will come up along the way. Getting past these problems is vital to teaching your team members a growth mindset. This means telling them to see problems as opportunities to learn and grow, not as impossible obstacles they can't overcome.

Turn your focus from "I can't" to "I can learn." Help your team members understand that failures are expected.

Remember, the best leaders are always learning. If you teach your team this growth attitude, they can better adapt, maintain resilience, and reach their full potential.

Open Communication

In addition to these strategies, having a culture of open communication is important. Make it a habit for your team members to ask you and their coworkers for comments.

Here's the key: Emphasize that feedback is not a personal attack but a valuable tool. Teams learn from receiving constructive feedback, focusing on the message, not the messenger. Remind your team of the importance of continuous career development. Encourage your team members to put effort into their learning by giving them tools, encouraging them to attend workshops or conferences, and giving them opportunities to use the new skills they've learned.

By using these tips, you will create a warm and welcoming space for your team to grow. You'll be amazed at the hidden skills you discover and the future leaders you help develop. Leaders include mentorship systems as a part of everyday life.

Senior leaders are paired with junior leaders in a general mentorship scheme. This allows veteran leaders to test their communication skills while passing valuable knowledge and experiences to newer team members. Here are some real-world steps you can take to make this powerful dynamic happen in your company:

1. Start at the Top

To build a strong mentorship culture, leaders must be committed to it. Leaders need to advocate for mentorship programs and show their support for them. This can be achieved through:

- Giving out resources: Set aside time and money for mentorship programs.

- Senior leaders can set a good example by being mentors themselves. This sends a strong message about the value of mentorship.
- Recognizing public mentorship relationships that work: Telling others about your successes can get more people to join.

2. The Right Pair

Compatibility is crucial to building the best mentorship ties. Experiment to avoid blindly pairing senior leaders with random subordinates. Pair teachers and mentees interested in or having goals in the same general area. Consider the following when pairing:

- Personalities: To find the right person, think about how they like to work and talk.
- Growth Mindset: Both teachers and mentees should want to learn and improve, specifically within a shared field of interest.

3. Structure the Mentorship

Mentorship relationships can be established casually but benefit from a reasonable structure. Consider outlining:

- Expectations and goals: What do both individuals want from this mentorship relationship?
- Number of Meetings: Set up regular check-in points to ensure growth and communication.
- Rules for communication: Choose your preferred communication methods and how you'd like to hear back. Establish guidelines for how you would like your team to communicate with others.

4. Formal Programs

Formal mentorship programs are excellent opportunities to promote growth and development within the team openly. Things to consider:

- Organize teams from different departments, if possible. Expanding and sharing an extensive knowledge base can set realistic expectations, clarify department priorities, and uncover valuable information.
- Create time for people to share what they know: Senior employees can share what they know at workshops or lunch-and-learns.

- New employees can be paired with more experienced coworkers who can help them become familiar with the company and its processes.

5. Recognize Success

It's important to recognize and celebrate the successes of good mentorship relationships. This could mean getting praise from the public, winning awards, or sharing good reviews. Leaders must encourage their mentees when they've hit that "Aha" moment. Mentors can be first-line cheerleaders as the mentee progresses in their field, congratulating them on their progress and a job well done. Mentorship culture will continue to sustain itself if you invest in the growth of both mentors and mentees.

Building a solid mentorship culture takes time and work, but the benefits are exponential. By making the workplace an environment of support, learning, and growth, you can get the most out of your team and make the workplace thrive.

Leading by example, encouraging growth, and cultivating a growth mindset are important ways to help the team create future leaders. Organizing official mentorship programs, encouraging casual mentorship opportunities, and celebrating successes are all ways to build a strong mentorship culture that encourages people to keep learning and working together.

Chapter 5

EMPOWERING OTHERS

Imagine a team where everyone feels valued, trusted, and empowered to contribute their best. This is not just an ideal but the reality of an empowered workplace. Empowering your team and new members or employees goes beyond delegation; it's about creating an environment that encourages them to take the initiative, feel capable of making decisions, and own their learning.

Why is empowerment so important in leadership development? It unleashes potential and fosters a positive work environment in the following ways:

1. Empowering Learning and Development

Micromanagement kills creativity and slows growth. Empowering junior leaders gives them the space to experiment, learn from their mistakes, and develop their skills.

Think about it; let them learn by managing projects or tasks. Then, they will be equipped to apply what they know to real situations and solve problems by themselves, developing their critical thinking. Hands-on experience speeds up growth and gets future leaders ready.

2. Trust and Collaboration

Empowerment builds trust within the team. When leaders demonstrate confidence in their team's abilities by delegating responsibilities, they pass a vital message: "I believe in you." This creates a psychologically safe environment where team members can take risks, share ideas, and collaborate effectively and securely.

Let's take this further: When trust is high, communication is open. Subordinates will feel free to ask their leaders for advice or questions. Open communication allows you to offer targeted support and creates a productive team where everyone is valued.

3. Motivation and Engagement

Empowering team members motivates and inspires them while making them feel like an all-too-small part of a larger system leads to disengagement. Empowerment inspires motivation and engagement. Giving junior leaders control over their work inspires a sense of belonging and motivates them to make a difference by giving their best.

Driven leaders are empowered leaders. Allow them to take pride in their achievement and see that their contribution is associated with the team's success. The feeling of purpose and ownership raises general engagement and motivation within the team.

Empowerment is not a one-time event; it is ongoing. Consider the following ideas as you develop:

Let individual junior leaders know exactly what they are expected to accomplish but not how. It's vital to be supportive and provide guidance but reinforce your confidence in them.

Be there when they have questions, need feedback, or require encouragement. Make yourself available.

Celebrate successes, big or small. Recognition will likely go a long way in building confidence and reinforcing positive behaviors.

Promote open communication. Create an environment where questions and feedback are welcomed.

Remember that when you empower your junior leaders, you do not lose control; instead, you create a culture of ownership, innovation, and shared success. This aids leadership development, builds a strong team, and ultimately better serves the organization.

What's Empowerment in Action?

We talked about empowerment and where it fits in leadership development. Now, let's pay closer attention and uncover practical strategies for empowering your team. Here's how you can ensure everyone feels valued, trusted, and empowered to give their best:

Matching Tasks with Skills

Effective delegation means assigning responsibilities that match individual strengths and development goals, not just dumping work on others. Analyze your team members' skills and experience. Delegate work that offers them the opportunity to learn and develop and matches their skill set.

Trust is the basis of empowerment. Start by delegating straightforward tasks, and gradually escalate complexity as your team becomes confident and mature. This will give them a sense of achievement and motivate them to get involved in more significant challenges.

Unleash Autonomy

Micromanagement is the enemy of empowerment. Empowering your team gives them the leeway to decide for themselves, take charge of problem-solving, and take control of their work.

Trust them to do things with little interference, showing your strong belief in their capability. This establishes ownership of the task and makes them even more motivated to do their best to succeed.

Of course, autonomy doesn't mean total isolation. Make your expectations and goals clear while allowing for flexibility in meeting them. Be available to help and guide, but don't hover and control every step.

Psychological Safety

Trust is the bedrock of a successful team, and empowerment builds trust through open communication. Encourage your team members to share ideas, concerns, and feedback freely. Be open to others' perspectives, practice active listening, and provide a safe space where others will be free to air their opinions, even if they differ from yours.

Psychological safety is non-negotiable. This means every team member feels safe taking appropriate risks, is vulnerable in admitting mistakes, and asks for help without fear of punishment or judgment. This opens communication lines and builds a trust climate where everyone feels valued and is free to give their best.

Work-Life Balance

When a team experiences burnout, productivity suffers. Burnout is a state of emotional, physical, and mental exhaustion caused by prolonged stress or continuous overwork. It can manifest as fatigue, cynicism, and a general sense of being overwhelmed. It is essential to recognize the signs of burnout and address them immediately. Ensure you set boundaries for your team, encourage them to seek support, and prioritize self-care.

Encouraging your team members to have a healthy work-life balance isn't a "nice" thing to do, but rather imperative for effective performance. Encourage your team to take breaks, use their vacation, and disconnect at the end of the working day. By respecting their personal life, you are letting your team know that you care about them and their well-being. Rested and recharged, the team comes back motivated, engaged, and ready to give their best.

Creating Opportunities for Collaboration

Collaboration involves teams pooling their resources, knowledge, and skills to tackle challenges through creative problem-solving. Structure your projects and tasks to encourage productive teamwork. Allow different people with different skills and backgrounds to work together.

Facilitating collaboration, knowledge-sharing, and innovation helps a team to achieve much more than a single person can. A strong team is greater than the sum of its parts.

Empowerment is a process, not an objective. These strategies will create a lively work environment where members feel valued, trusted, and encouraged to be their best. This results in a culture of ownership and innovation, ultimately improving the organization.

Human Resource Development:

Continuous training and development are among the most effective ways to empower your team.

This can be achieved via:

- **Formal Training Programs:** Provide opportunities for your employees to learn new skills and gain knowledge relevant to their roles.
- **Mentorship Programs:** Pair your team members with experienced mentors who can provide guidance, support, or career advice.
- **Coaching:** Invest in programs where your team is coached to develop certain skills or overcome specific challenges.

However, before we examine these development strategies in detail, let's highlight three key roles that can be vital in growing your team: mentors, coaches, and teachers.

1. Mentors

A mentor is a trusted adviser or role model who typically has experience working in the field and provides long-term guidance and support. It can be an informal relationship created mainly through mutual trust and respect. A mentor can advise on how to advance one's career and assist in navigating the difficulties and opportunities in the organization and beyond.

2. Coaches

Coaches are facilitators who focus on professional and personal growth. They work mainly with individuals or teams in a more structured manner than the mentor. Coaches focus on developing skills or accomplishing goals. Coaches should utilize various approaches, as mentioned previously in this book, to unlock the potential of their team members and enable them to achieve their desired goals. The relationship with coaches is typically collaborative, with coaches acting more as guides or facilitators instead of traditional authoritative figures.

3. Teachers

Like coaches, teachers are charged with the improvement of knowledge or skills. They often do their work in the classroom, using methodology to deliver specific knowledge or skills to learners. Teachers might contribute to the development process, but this is less through knowledge transfer and more through mentorship or coaching. The relationship between teachers and students is often hierarchical, with teachers holding authority instead of being viewed as peers.

You can leverage mentors, coaches, and teachers' unique roles in developing a holistic plan for your team's development.

Empowered Leaders to Make a Difference

Empowerment is not a new term in management. Instead, it enables development and creates an innovative team environment. Unlocking the value of trust and confidence in team members lies in empowering capabilities to immense potential and then unleashing positive outcomes.

Investing in the development of team members is investing in the organization's future. Allocating resources toward individuals' growth contributes to your team's growth. Thus, equipping team members with the requisite skills and knowledge will empower them, give them a sense of ownership, help them work better together, and yield phenomenal results.

Chapter 6

CREATING A LEADERSHIP PIPELINE

Leaders create leaders. Consider a thriving organization where talented individuals are encouraged to take leadership roles. This isn't a pipe dream; it's the reality of a company with a strong leadership pipeline. Like any thriving garden, your organization needs a plan to nurture future leaders, ensuring a steady stream of talent to guide your company toward a bright future. There is an oak in every acorn.

So, how do you cultivate a strong leadership pipeline?

Here are some key strategies you implement:

Identifying Leadership Competencies

The first step is defining leadership in your organization. What are the core competencies successful leaders embody? These might include communication skills, strategic thinking, problem-solving abilities, and the capacity to inspire and motivate others. What does your organization need in a leader?

Consider this: You wouldn't plant seeds without knowing what flowers you want to grow. Similarly, by defining your ideal leadership profile, you can identify individuals with the potential to blossom into future leaders.

Refrain from solely relying on titles or experience; look for individuals who demonstrate desired competencies in their current roles. Observe how they handle challenges, interact with colleagues, and motivate those around them. Identify those who do not blame their circumstances but use them to their advantage.

Regular Talent Assessments

Identifying potential leaders isn't a one-time event. Regular talent assessments are crucial for gauging an individual's growth trajectory and leadership potential.

These assessments shouldn't be intimidating or punitive. They should be seen as opportunities for growth and development. Utilize various assessment tools, including self-assessments, 360-degree feedback, and performance reviews. Document your observations and assessments to track individual progress and identify areas for targeted development. Make time for these assessments and schedule reviews often.

Creating Success Plans for Junior Leaders

Once you've identified high-potential individuals, collaborate with them to create personalized success plans. These plans should outline their career goals and the steps to achieve them. Individualized plans develop your leaders and yield a much more significant return.

This is a roadmap. Include specific development opportunities like training programs, mentorship relationships, or stretch assignments. Review and adjust these plans as needed regularly to ensure they align with individual aspirations and organizational needs.

Leadership Development Opportunities

Empowerment is vital to fostering leadership growth. Provide junior leaders with a variety of leadership development opportunities. Although they will require guidance during their leadership development, they must be free to make mistakes.

These could include:

- **Formal training programs:** Equip them with the skills and knowledge they need to be successful leaders (e.g., communication skills, negotiation techniques, strategic thinking).
- **Mentorship programs:** Connect them with experienced mentors who can offer guidance, support, and insights.
- **Coaching programs:** Invest in coaching that helps them develop specific leadership skills or overcome challenges.
- **Conferences and workshops:** Expose them to new ideas and best practices in leadership. Consider bringing in outside spokespersons to provide new perspectives.

Ensure these speakers align with the values of the organization.

By providing these opportunities, you demonstrate your commitment to their growth and invest in your organization's future.

Stretch Assignments to Push Potential

Growth often happens outside our comfort zones. "Stretch assignments" are challenging projects or tasks that push junior leaders to develop new skills and expand their leadership capabilities. These assignments are often just beyond their typical scope of duties, so encourage your team to practice achieving more challenging tasks.

Assigning a high-potential team member to lead a cross-functional project allows them to develop their communication, collaboration, and problem-solving skills in a real-world setting. These experiences build their confidence and showcase their leadership potential to the broader organization.

Remember, effective leadership development is an ongoing process. By implementing these strategies, you can cultivate a strong leadership pipeline that ensures a steady stream of talented individuals ready to take the reins and guide your organization toward continued success.

Transforming High-Performers into Leaders

We've established the importance of a strong leadership pipeline. Now, let's dig deeper and highlight specific strategies for identifying high-potential employees and nurturing them into future leaders:

1. Identifying High-Potential Employees

Not all high performers are cut out for leadership. Although past achievements are significant, look for individuals who exhibit the core competencies defined in your leadership profile. Said plainly, identify individuals who want to lead. That said, do not discourage high performers from leadership development opportunities; they will blossom when ready.

Here are some questions when considering critical indicators of leadership potential:

- **Initiative:** Do they take ownership and go above and beyond their assigned tasks?
- **Problem-solving skills:** Can they approach challenges creatively and find practical solutions?

- **Communication skills:** Can they clearly articulate ideas, inspire others, and build consensus?
- **Collaboration:** Do they work effectively with team members from diverse backgrounds?
- **Learning agility:** Are they open to new ideas and willing to continuously learn and grow?

Look for individuals who consistently answer these questions, not just in their current roles but also in their outside endeavors. This also requires you to know your team personally and professionally.

2. Cross-departmental Rotation

While working alone is valuable, isolation within an organization can hinder growth. One powerful strategy for developing future leaders is by implementing cross-departmental rotation. Also known as job rotation, this practice allows team members to understand the organization's objectives, develop diverse skills, and build relationships with other teams.

Assigning a high-potential employee to work on a project in a different department exposes them to new perspectives, broader organizational knowledge, and diverse leadership styles. This enhances their skillset and allows them to identify opportunities for collaboration and innovation across departments.

Cross-training is equally valuable. Providing opportunities for employees to learn new skills outside their immediate roles equips them with a broader skillset and prepares them for future leadership opportunities.

3. Fostering Continuous Learning

Leaders are lifelong learners. Fostering a culture of continuous learning within your organization is a crucial aspect of leadership development. The desire to learn more can display proactivity and commitment to self-development.

Embrace the mantra "Do good things and never stop learning!" Encourage your team members, especially high-potential individuals, to actively seek learning opportunities. This could involve attending conferences, pursuing professional development courses, or participating in online learning platforms.

By providing access to learning resources and encouraging a growth mindset, you empower your team to reach their full potential.

4. Evaluation and Adjustment

Development is an ongoing process. Regularly evaluate the progress of your high-potential employees. Utilize performance reviews, 360-degree feedback, and informal check-ins to assess their growth and identify areas for further development.

Leaders must be adaptable, including you. Adjust your leadership development strategies based on individual needs and changing circumstances; a practice known as self-monitoring. The key is to ensure your high-potential employees are continuously challenged and supported on their leadership journey.

5. Succession Planning

Leadership development isn't just about identifying potential; it's about ensuring a smooth transition for future leadership roles. Succession planning is an essential component of a robust leadership pipeline.

Interact with your high-potential employees to identify their career aspirations and prospective leadership positions. Based on your findings, develop a personalized succession plan that outlines the steps they need to take to prepare for those roles.

Succession planning should include:

- Targeted training programs to develop specific skills.
- Mentorship from experienced leaders.
- Participation in strategic decision-making processes.
- Opportunities to lead and manage projects.

Implementing these strategies can help identify high-potential employees, provide them with the tools and support they need to grow, and ensure a smooth transition to future leadership roles. This, in turn, fosters organizational stability and paves the way for long-term success.

Building a strong leadership pipeline is an investment in your organization's future. By nurturing high-potential employees and fostering a culture of continuous learning, you create fertile ground for future leaders to blossom and guide your company toward a brighter tomorrow.

Building a Leadership Pipeline for Enduring Success: A Practical Guide

We've discussed the importance of training future leaders and the critical strategies for identifying and developing high-potential employees. Now, let's get practical and outline a step-by-step approach to building a robust leadership pipeline that ensures long-term success for your organization:

Phase 1: Laying the Foundation (Planning Your Pipeline)

Understanding the Managerial Landscape:

- Management plays a crucial role in steering an organization towards its goals. Managers make decisions, allocate resources, and motivate teams to achieve desired outcomes. They act as a bridge between strategy and execution.
- Effective decision-making is a cornerstone of successful management. Understanding the managerial decision-making process is crucial. This involves identifying problems, analyzing options, selecting the best action, and implementing the solution.
- The competitive environment significantly impacts strategic decision-making. When charting their course, organizations must consider external factors like competitor strategies, industry trends, and customer demands.
- Strategic planning is a crucial process that outlines your organization's long-term direction. Understanding its

fundamental principles will help you establish a leadership pipeline aligning with your business strategy.

Phase 2: Building a Strong Structure (Organizing Your Pipeline)

Navigating Internal and External Forces:

- Both internal and external factors influence organizational planning, strategy, and change. Internal factors like company culture, leadership styles, and resource availability must be considered. External such as economic conditions, technological advancements, and government regulations also play a significant role. Effectively navigating these factors requires flexibility and adaptability. Your leadership development strategy should be able to accommodate changes in the internal and external landscapes.
- International Management and Globalization: Understanding how businesses operate globally and their impact on worldwide connections cannot be overemphasized. To train future leaders and provide opportunities to experience diverse cultures and global perspectives. Encourage diversity within your team to

promote inclusivity and creative problem-solving. With the advent of technology, we are more connected than ever before. Remind your team of the importance of professional connections and diversity.

- Organizational Structures and Diversity: There are diverse organizational structures, such as hierarchical, flat, and matrix. Consider the structure that best promotes leadership development in your organization.

Remember, diversity is a strength. Fostering a diverse leadership pipeline taps into a wider talent pool and benefits from a broader range of perspectives and experiences.

Phase 3: Developing Great Leaders (Leading Your Pipeline)

Developing Effective Leaders:

- Leadership traits and best practices are essential for a strong leadership pipeline. Identify the specific leadership qualities your organization values most. This might include communication skills, strategic thinking, emotional intelligence, and the ability to inspire and motivate others.

- Motivation is the driving force behind human behavior. Understanding significant theories of human motivation will equip you to create a leadership development program that fosters engagement and high performance. By understanding your team and what drives their success, you will be better equipped to motivate junior leaders during their training.
- Mid-level and low-level leaders are the backbone of a team. Recognize the role and importance of teams in your organization and ensure your leadership pipeline includes opportunities for developing strong team leadership skills. These leaders have experience in the conceptual and practical implementation of an organization's objectives.
- Effective communication is necessary for successful leadership. Ensure your leadership training and development programs focus on improving communication skills. Leaders should clearly express a vision and give clear instructions. Doing so helps build trust through open and honest communication.

Phase 4: Continuous Improvement (Controlling/Assessing Your Pipeline)

Monitoring and Measuring Success:

- Management control systems help ensure organizational goals are being met. Implementing relevant control systems lets you track your leadership pipeline's progress and identify improvement areas. This could be as simple as weekly, handwritten reviews or as complex as an elaborate spreadsheet.
- Information technology (IT) is vital in modern management practices. Use technology to make the development process more efficient, allow employees access to learning resources, and track the progress of your high-potential employees.
- Optimizing Human Capital: Your people are your greatest asset. Invest in strategies to manage and optimize human capital within your organization. This includes talent acquisition, training and development, and performance management practices that support your leadership pipeline.
- Ethical Leadership: Leaders set the tone for the entire organization. Building a leadership pipeline requires emphasizing the importance of ethical leadership and management.

Following these steps and improving your approach will build a strong leadership pipeline that nurtures the continuous flow of skilled and ethical leaders. This positions your company for continued growth and prosperity in a constantly evolving world. Remember, ethical leaders act with integrity, fairness, and transparency. They build trust and inspire others to do the same.

Chapter 7

MANAGING CONFLICT AND PERSONALITY CLASHES

Have you ever felt at war with yourself? Maybe you're wrestling with a decision or stressed about competing priorities. Perhaps you constantly clash with a coworker or feel frustrated in your relationships. Conflict internal and external is a normal part of life. But navigating these challenges can make a big difference to our well-being and the health of our connections.

This chapter will equip you with the tools to understand and effectively resolve conflict.

Decoding Conflict: Inner and Outer Battles

Inner Conflict: This is the struggle that happens within us. It could be the voice telling you to eat healthily while you crave dessert or the anxiety about an upcoming presentation. Inner conflict can be a source of stress and anxiety, but it can also be an opportunity for personal growth. By acknowledging these internal battles and analyzing their roots, we can make choices that align with our values and goals. To face our inner conflict is confronting and effectively dealing with the problem – as leaders do.

Outer Conflict: This is the disagreement between you and others. It can happen with friends, family, colleagues, or even strangers. Misunderstandings, differences in opinion, or competition for resources can cause outer conflict. While possibly disruptive, it can also lead to stronger relationships and innovative solutions if addressed constructively. Use outer conflict to practice communication, transparency, and professionalism.

Theories to Guide Our Actions

Various theories explore the nature and resolution of conflict. Understanding these critical concepts can help us approach conflict more calmly.

The Stages of Conflict: A Brewing Storm

Conflict doesn't erupt overnight. It often follows a predictable pattern with distinct stages:

1. **Latent Conflict:** This is the underlying issue or tension that has yet to surface. For example, a feeling of resentment might simmer beneath the surface in a relationship.
2. **Perceived Conflict:** The issue becomes apparent, and one or both parties recognize a disagreement.
3. **Felt Conflict:** Emotions escalate as the parties become aware of the threat to their needs or desires.
4. **Manifest Conflict:** The disagreement becomes overt, with arguments, accusations, or withdrawal. This is when feelings become hurt, upsetting words are exchanged, and relationships can be damaged.
5. **Outcome:** This is the resolution, which can be positive, negative, or unresolved. Typically, if left unattended, the outcome of heated conflicts results in a long-lasting negative view of the other party.

By recognizing the stages of conflict, we can intervene early, preventing a minor disagreement from escalating into a full-blown fight.

Navigating Conflict Styles: Finding Your Voice

People approach conflict differently. Here, we'll highlight five common conflict styles.

- **Competing:** This assertive style prioritizes winning and may involve forceful arguments.
- **Avoiding:** This passive style involves withdrawing from the conflict altogether.
- **Compromising:** This involves seeking a middle ground where both parties give up something.
- **Accommodating:** This passive style prioritizes the other person's needs over your own.
- **Collaborating:** This assertive and cooperative style aims for a win-win solution that addresses everyone's concerns.

Understanding your conflict style and those of the people you interact with can help you choose the most effective approach for resolving disagreements.

Major Processes for Resolution: Tools for Peace

There are various methods for resolving conflict, some of which we'll explain in detail later. The most common tools for resolution include:

1. **Negotiation:** This involves a structured conversation to reach a mutually agreeable solution. Leaders should be comfortable negotiating professionally and calmly.
2. **Mediation:** A neutral third party facilitates communication and helps the conflicting parties find common ground.
3. **Problem-solving:** This approach focuses on identifying the underlying issue and working together to find a solution that benefits everyone.

By equipping yourself with these conflict resolution strategies, you'll be better prepared to resolve disagreements confidently and find solutions that foster stronger relationships and personal growth.

Fundamentals of Conflict: Diving Deeper

Now that we've discussed the different types and stages of conflict, let's analyze the core factors determining how we react or respond to conflict.

1. **The Mind's Role in Conflict:** Our thoughts significantly influence how we perceive and react to conflict. Negative biases and assumptions about the other person's intentions can fuel escalation. Conversely, practicing mindfulness and reframing situations in a more positive light can help us approach conflict with a calmer and more open mind. Albeit challenging, leaders must attempt to understand their biases when approaching conflict and view the situation objectively.
2. **Physiology and Conflict:** Our bodies react to conflict in real time. Increased heart rate, muscle tension, and sweating are all signs of the body's fight-or-flight response. Learning to manage these physiological responses through relaxation techniques like deep breathing can help us stay grounded and communicate effectively during conflict. Regardless, we must always refrain from physical explosiveness when in a professional environment.

3. **Emotions and Conflict:** It's natural to feel various emotions during conflict, including anger, frustration, or fear. However, allowing emotions to control our communication can lead to regrettable outbursts. Recognizing and acknowledging our feelings enables us to express them constructively and avoid emotional manipulation. As a leader, it's best to remember that your team always observes how you manage your emotions in difficult situations.
4. **Impact of Conflict on Relationships:** The nature of our relationship with the other person significantly impacts how we approach conflict. Similarly, our approach to conflict will affect our relationships. We might be more willing to engage in open and honest communication with close friends or family. In professional settings, maintaining professional boundaries must be a priority. Consider the nature of the conflict and how it may change the dynamic of your relationship. Don't be afraid to stake your case, but winning a battle doesn't mean you've won the war.
5. **Core Needs and Concerns in Conflict:** Unmet needs and concerns lie at the heart of most conflicts. Identifying these underlying issues is crucial for finding a solution that

addresses everyone's core desires. For example, disagreements between colleagues might stem from a need for recognition or a desire for more transparent communication. Conflict is most efficiently understood when leaders identify and separate the behavior from the person.

6. **The Communication Process in Conflict**

   Effective communication is paramount for resolving conflicts constructively. Here, we'll break down the critical steps in communication and how to apply them during conflict:

   1. Steps in the Communication Process:

- **Sending:** Clearly articulating your thoughts, feelings, and needs.
- **Encoding:** Choosing appropriate words and non-verbal cues to convey your message accurately.
- **Transmission:** Delivering your message through a channel (verbal, written, etc.).
- **Decoding:** The receiver interprets your message based on their own experiences and biases.

- **Receiving:** The receiver actively listens and understands your message.
- **Feedback:** The receiver provides a response that indicates their understanding of your message.

2. Application in Conflict Situations:

- Active Listening: Pay close attention to the other person's verbal and non-verbal messages. Avoid interrupting and focus on understanding their perspective.
- "I" Statements: Use "I" statements to express your feelings and needs without blaming the other person. For example, "I feel frustrated when..." instead of "You always..."
- Non-verbal Communication: Maintain eye contact, use open body language, and speak calmly and respectfully.

By understanding these fundamentals of conflict, you'll be better equipped to resolve disagreements calmly, communicate effectively, and ultimately find solutions that foster healthier relationships and personal growth.

Conflict Resolution Skills: Turning Conflict into Collaboration

Now that we know the underlying dynamics of conflict let's learn the skills needed to resolve disagreements constructively and reach win-win solutions.

Active Communication Methods for Conflict Resolution

Active communication is the pillar of effective conflict resolution. Here are some essential methods to implement:

- **Clarifying Questions:** Ask open-ended questions to better understand the other person's perspective. For example, "Can you tell me more about what you're feeling frustrated about?"
- **Paraphrasing:** Restate the other person's message in your own words to demonstrate understanding. This can help to identify any miscommunication and ensure you're both on the same page.
- **Validating Feelings:** Acknowledge the other person's emotions, even if you disagree. This helps to build trust and create a safe space for open communication. For

example, "It sounds like you're feeling disrespected. I can understand why that would be frustrating."

Differentiating Between Positions and Interests

During conflict, it's essential to differentiate between positions (stated demands) and interests (underlying needs). Positions often represent a solution, while interests represent the core desires a solution should address. For example, in a work disagreement, your position might be, "I need this report finished by tomorrow." However, your underlying interest might be efficiency or a desire to avoid last-minute stress. Focusing on interests allows for a more collaborative approach to finding solutions that address everyone's needs.

Strategies for Addressing Underlying Needs

Once you've identified the underlying interests in a conflict, you can start brainstorming solutions that address them. Here are some strategies:

- **Brainstorming:** Work together to generate various potential solutions without judgment or criticism.

- **Creative Problem-solving:** Think outside the box and explore unconventional solutions that might not have been considered initially.
- **Finding Common Ground:** Look for areas of agreement, even if they seem small. This can help to build momentum and foster a more collaborative spirit.

Win-Win Thinking and Application

A win-win approach to conflict resolution prioritizes finding a solution that benefits everyone involved. This doesn't necessarily mean that everyone gets exactly what they want, but rather that everyone's core needs are addressed to some degree. By focusing on win-win solutions, you can build stronger relationships, create a more positive work environment, and foster a sense of shared success.

Steps for Developing Practical Solutions

Here's a breakdown of the critical steps to follow when developing practical solutions:

1. **Understanding Underlying Needs:** Identify the core interests and needs driving the conflict for all parties involved.
2. **Win-Win Problem Solving:** Brainstorm solutions that address the underlying needs identified in step 1. Prioritize solutions that create a win-win scenario for everyone involved.
3. **Active Communication:** Clearly and collaboratively communicate proposed solutions and ensure everyone involved feels heard and understood. Be prepared to adapt solutions based on feedback and ongoing communication.

By mastering these conflict resolution skills and following the steps outlined above, you'll be well-equipped to effectively resolve disagreements, build stronger relationships, and find solutions that foster a more positive and productive environment.

Putting Conflict Resolution into Action: From Theory to Practice

Now that you have the knowledge and skills for effective conflict resolution, how do you apply them to real-world situations?

A. The Conflict Analysis Process: Unpacking the Issue

Before diving into solutions, a thorough analysis of the conflict is crucial. Here's a breakdown of the critical steps and considerations:

- **Step 1: Gather Information:** Collect details about the conflict, including the people involved, the situation that triggered it, and the desired outcomes for each party.
- **Step 2: Identify Underlying Needs and Interests:** Uncover the core desires and concerns driving the conflict for everyone involved.
- **Step 3: Analyze Communication Styles:** Identify the communication styles of those involved and any potential communication gaps that might hinder progress.
- **Step 4: Consider Power Dynamics:** Be mindful of any power imbalances between the people in conflict. This

awareness can help ensure a fair and balanced resolution process.

B. Conflict Resolution Process Design: Crafting a Roadmap

Once you've thoroughly analyzed the conflict, you can design a resolution process. Here are the key steps and considerations:

- **Step 1: Establish Ground Rules:** Set clear expectations for respectful communication, active listening, and a focus on finding solutions rather than assigning blame.
- **Step 2: Facilitation:** Decide whether a neutral third party can facilitate the conversation or if the parties involved will manage it themselves. A facilitator can help maintain a constructive dialogue and ensure all voices are heard.
- **Step 3: Brainstorming Solutions:** Work collaboratively to generate various potential solutions that address the underlying needs identified in the analysis phase.
- **Step 4: Evaluation and Selection:** Evaluate each proposed solution based on its effectiveness in meeting

everyone's needs and overall feasibility. Select the solution that best represents a win-win scenario.

- **Step 5: Implementation and Follow-up:** Develop a clear plan for implementing the chosen solution. Schedule follow-up meetings to monitor progress and address any new challenges that might arise.

C. Application in Real-World Scenarios

Conflict resolution skills are valuable in various settings. Here are some examples:

- **Workplace Disputes:** Use these skills to navigate disagreements with colleagues, resolve team conflicts, and constructively address performance issues.
- **Family Relationships:** Effective communication fosters stronger family bonds. Use these methods to address disagreements with parents, siblings, or children healthily and respectfully.
- **Social Conflicts:** These skills can mediate disagreements with friends or navigate challenging social situations.

D. Emerging Applications in Various Contexts

The principles of conflict resolution extend beyond personal interactions. They can be applied to:

- **Community Mediation:** Trained facilitators can resolve community conflicts, fostering peace and understanding.
- **International Relations:** Conflict resolution skills are crucial in diplomacy and nation negotiations.
- **Organizational Development:** These skills can create a more collaborative and productive work environment.

Developing your conflict resolution skills increases your mediation abilities and knowledge of how to apply them in different contexts. This will help you contribute significantly to a more peaceful and collaborative world, whether personally or professionally.

Conflict doesn't need to be a destructive force. By understanding its nature, developing effective communication skills, and following a structured conflict resolution process, we can turn conflicts into opportunities for growth, build stronger relationships, and inspire positive change.

Abraham Lincoln stated, "The best way to resolve a conflict is to avoid it. The second best is to resolve it quickly."

This chapter has taught you the skills and tools to effectively mediate conflicts, prevent unnecessary escalation, and propose solutions that foster a more peaceful and collaborative world. Remember, conflict resolution is a skill that takes practice and refinement. By continuously honing these skills and approaching conflict with an open mind and a willingness to collaborate, you can contribute to building a more harmonious world.

Chapter 8

BUILDING RESILIENCE IN LEADERS

Change and challenges have one thing in common – they are inevitable in life's journey. Challenges do not define us, but rather how we react to them. This is especially true when it comes to leadership. Every leader must build resiliency; it is the key to building and maintaining success.

Resilience is the ability to recover from adversity swiftly; it is a type of mental toughness that allows people to bounce back from setbacks and keep going forward. Resilience is not only desirable in leaders but also a core requirement. From handling team dynamics to making tough choices under pressure, the path to leadership is filled with challenges. It takes resilience and determination for a leader to navigate turbulent times gracefully.

Why is resilience so important for leaders? Consider all the duties and stress they are under. Leaders are usually expected to make tough decisions, take risks, and show their people the way. Their calm and collected demeanor significantly influenced their team's mood and performance during chaotic times. A resilient leader can instill trust and security even in the most trying situations.

A positive mindset shift is the first step toward resilience. It involves seeing challenges as opportunities to grow rather than insurmountable barriers. By adopting this perspective, leaders can embrace change and uncertainty instead of being afraid of them. It encourages proactive solutions to problems instead of dwelling on the challenge.

Attention to self-care and balance is another quality of a resilient leader. Taking care of yourself is not a luxury; it is a necessity. The demands of leadership are sometimes overwhelming, thus creating the necessity of setting healthy boundaries, taking care of your health, and making time for rest and relaxation. The consequence of not taking care of your health is burnout, which makes it challenging to make effective decisions and significantly reduces productivity.

Building resilience also means being part of a strong support network. No one should have to deal with problems alone. Having a team of trusted coworkers, experts, and friends can be very helpful. These relationships provide benefits such as brainstorming ideas, getting support, and reminding you that you're not alone in your struggles.

Learning from mistakes is another essential aspect of resilience. Failure is a part of life, and as leaders, how we handle it is what counts. Resilient leaders view failure as an opportunity to learn, not a sign of their worth. They analyze what went wrong, learn from it, and then apply what they've learned to new challenges. The critical feature that distinguishes resilient leaders from others is their ability to adapt and change.

Keeping an upbeat attitude is essential, even when things don't go as planned. There is no need to ignore the truth about adverse circumstances. Instead, focus on the positive outcomes that might occur. Being positive helps leaders and their teams stay inspired.

A strong sense of purpose is also essential for resilience. As a leader, being clear about your morals and goals will help you stay focused and committed, even when things get tough. Having a sense of purpose is like having a guiding star. When the future seems uncertain, it shows you the way and keeps you going.

Resilience is a skill that requires intentional effort, constant practice, willingness to leave your comfort zone, and a commitment to personal improvement. People who want to be leaders will do better at developing their resilience. This will help them face the challenges of leadership with confidence and authority.

In a nutshell, a strong leader must be resilient. It helps leaders deal with challenges, motivate their teams, and stay healthy. Resilient leaders ensure they not only survive but thrive in their jobs. This way, they are prepared to lead with determination and conviction, no matter what comes their way. Remember that resilience is more than getting back up after a setback; it also means going forward with more strength and wisdom.

Building Resilience as a Leader

Leadership isn't always sunshine and smooth sailing. It's about navigating choppy waters, making tough decisions, and facing challenges head-on. This is where resilience comes in. Resilient leaders can bounce back from setbacks, learn from adversity, and emerge stronger.

So, how do you cultivate this essential quality? Here are some key strategies to build resilience as a leader:

Reframe Challenges as Opportunities

The first step is acknowledging that challenges are inevitable, irrespective of your skills or success level.

The key is to shift your perspective. Instead of viewing challenges as insurmountable obstacles, see them as opportunities for growth. Ask yourself, "What can I learn from this experience?" "How can I use this to become a better leader?"

Remember: Leaders who embrace challenges and see them as learning opportunities not only develop their skills but also inspire their teams to do the same.

Develop Healthy Coping Mechanisms

Leaders are human, and it's okay to feel stressed or overwhelmed. The key is to deal with these emotions using healthy coping mechanisms constructively. Here are a few suggestions:

- Physical activity: Exercise is a powerful stress reliever. Regular physical activity releases endorphins, which improve mood and reduce stress hormones.
- Practice mindfulness: Techniques like meditation or deep breathing can help you center yourself during stressful situations. Taking a few minutes to focus on your breath and quiet your mind significantly improves your ability to manage stress.
- Social support: Don't go it alone. Build a strong support network of colleagues, friends, or a mentor you can confide in and seek advice from during challenging times.
- Creative outlets: Engaging in activities you enjoy, whether writing, painting, playing music, or spending time in nature, helps you de-stress and recharge.

Healthy coping mechanisms allow you to manage stress effectively, preventing it from clouding your judgment or hindering your ability to lead your team.

The Power of Self-Care

Leaders who neglect self-care are setting themselves up for burnout. Taking care of yourself isn't selfish; it's essential for maintaining your physical and mental well-being, allowing you to be a more effective leader.

Here are some self-care practices to consider:

- Get enough sleep: Aim for 7-8 hours of quality sleep each night. Sleep deprivation can significantly impair your mood, focus, and decision-making abilities.
- Eat healthy: Nourishing your body with nutritious foods provides the energy and focus you need to tackle challenges.
- Set boundaries: Learn to say no and delegate tasks effectively. Don't overload yourself; setting boundaries and prioritizing your well-being is okay.
- Schedule time for relaxation: Make time for activities that bring you joy and relaxation. These could include reading, spending time with loved ones, or taking a relaxing bath.

Self-care isn't a luxury; it's a necessity. Prioritizing your well-being equips you to handle leadership demands and inspires your team to do the same.

Embrace Reflection and Growth

Everyone makes mistakes. Resilient leaders don't dwell on failures; they learn from them. After a setback, take some time to reflect on what happened. Ask yourself:

- What went wrong?
- What could I have done differently?
- What can I learn from this experience?

By actively seeking lessons from setbacks, you can use them as steppingstones for future growth.

Cultivating Optimism and Hope

Resilient leaders are optimistic. They believe in themselves, their team, and their ability to overcome challenges. This positive outlook is contagious and inspires others to persevere through difficult times.

Hope is another essential component of resilience. Even in the face of adversity, believe that things will get better.

Remember: Challenges are temporary, but your ability to overcome them is a testament to your strength and resilience.

Developing resilience as a leader is a continuous process. By incorporating these strategies into your daily life, you'll develop the strength and fortitude to navigate challenges, overcome setbacks, and emerge a more decisive, effective leader. You'll be better equipped to weather the storms of leadership and guide your team toward success, even in adversity.

Remember, leadership isn't about invincibility; it's about adaptability and resourcefulness. It's about learning from experience, bouncing back from setbacks, and inspiring your team to do the same. By cultivating resilience, you become a beacon of strength and stability for those you lead, fostering a more positive and productive work environment for everyone.

Using real-life examples and case studies, I will demonstrate how resilience enables leaders to overcome obstacles and thrive despite adversity.

Howard Schultz

Howard Schultz, the former CEO of Starbucks, is another compelling example of resilience. Schultz grew up in a poor neighborhood in Brooklyn, New York, and faced numerous hardships during childhood. Despite these early challenges, he worked his way up through determination and resilience.

When Schultz took over Starbucks, the company was struggling. He implemented a bold vision to transform the coffee culture in America, focusing on creating a unique customer experience. Schultz faced skepticism and resistance from stakeholders. During the 2008 financial crisis, Starbucks experienced a severe downturn, leading to store closures and layoffs.

However, Schultz remained resilient and focused on innovation, improving employee welfare, and maintaining a strong company culture – this played a vital role in Starbucks' resurgence and growth into a global brand.

Malala Yousafzai

Malala Yousafzai, the youngest Nobel Prize laureate, is a remarkable example of resilience. As an advocate for girls' education in Pakistan, Malala faced life-threatening opposition from the Taliban. In 2012, she survived an assassination attempt that left her critically injured.

Despite this horrific experience, Malala's resilience and determination to fight for education grew stronger. After her recovery, she continued her activism on an even larger scale, using her platform to advocate for girls' education globally. Her courage and resilience have inspired millions around the world, leading to significant advancements in education for girls in many countries.

Malala's story proves that resilience empowers individuals to overcome even the most harrowing obstacles and turn personal adversity into a powerful force for global change.

Reed Hastings

Reed Hastings, the co-founder and CEO of Netflix, is a resilient business innovator. In the early 2000s, Netflix faced significant challenges as a DVD rental service, especially with the advent of digital streaming. Hastings boldly pivoted the company's business model from DVD rentals to online streaming.

This transition came with its challenges. The company faced substantial financial risks, technological hurdles, and skepticism from investors and customers. However, Hastings' forward-thinking approach allowed Netflix to navigate these obstacles. He focused on long-term goals, embraced new technologies, and continually adapted the company's strategy to stay ahead of the competition.

Today, Netflix is a leading global streaming service, revolutionizing the entertainment industry. Hastings' resilience and willingness to take calculated risks have been instrumental in Netflix's success.

Oprah Winfrey

Oprah Winfrey's journey from a troubled childhood to becoming a media mogul is a testament to resilience. Growing up in poverty and facing numerous personal challenges, including abuse and discrimination, Winfrey's path to success was far from easy.

Despite these adversities, Winfrey's resilience propelled her forward. She pursued her passion for media and worked her way up in the television industry. Her breakthrough came with "The Oprah Winfrey Show," one of the highest-rated talk shows in television history.

Winfrey's resilience is evident in her ability to overcome personal and professional challenges, maintain her authenticity, and continuously innovate. She has built a media empire, launched successful ventures like OWN (Oprah Winfrey Network), and become a global influencer.

Winfrey's story illustrates how resilience can help leaders overcome obstacles, build successful careers, and profoundly impact the world.

Leadership is filled with inevitable challenges, but leaders' resilience enables them to navigate these obstacles and emerge stronger. Through the inspiring examples of the successes of Howard Schultz, Malala Yousafzai, Reed Hastings, and Oprah Winfrey, we see how resilience helps leaders overcome adversity, stay true to their principles, and achieve outstanding success.

By adopting a growth mindset, practicing healthy coping mechanisms, prioritizing self-care, building strong support networks, and embracing continuous learning, leaders can cultivate the resilience necessary to face any challenge head-on and inspire their teams to do the same.

As you strive to become a resilient leader, remember John Quincy Adams's words: “If your actions inspire others to dream more, learn more, do more, and become more, you are a leader.” As you lead with determination, strength, and unwavering conviction, let resilience be your guide.

Chapter 9

SUSTAINING MOTIVATION AND ENGAGEMENT

As I write this final chapter, I can't help but reflect on the journey we've taken together. Leadership is a marathon, not a sprint; staying motivated and committed over the long haul is crucial for success. In this chapter, I will share key strategies I've learned and observed that can help keep the fire burning in your heart and mind.

Being a leader isn't always glamorous. It is often a thankless job. There are days you feel on top of the world, and other days when you question why you ever took the role. That's normal. What matters is how you navigate those ups and downs and keep yourself and your team moving forward.

Recognizing and Rewarding Achievement

One of the most powerful tools in a leader's arsenal is recognizing and rewarding productive efforts. It's not just about handing out bonuses or plaques (though those can be nice). It's about creating a culture where people feel seen and valued for their contributions.

Start small. Make it a habit to catch people doing things right. A simple "Great job on that presentation" or "I noticed how you handled that difficult customer – well done" can go a long way. These moments of recognition don't cost a dime, but they're worth their weight in gold regarding motivation.

But don't stop there. Get creative with your rewards. Maybe it's a coveted monthly parking spot, an extra day off, or the chance to lead an exciting new project. The key is to make the reward meaningful to the individual. One size doesn't fit all when it comes to recognition.

Document these wins. Keep a "wins" journal. At the end of each week, jot down a few notable achievements from your team. This helps you remember to recognize people and gives you a powerful tool for performance reviews and building team morale.

Remember, as a leader, you need recognition too. Don't be afraid to celebrate your own big and small wins. Share them with your mentor or a trusted colleague. Acknowledging your own progress is essential for maintaining your motivation.

Fostering a Sense of Purpose and Belonging

Let's talk about purpose. We all want to feel like our work matters, right? As a leader, one of your most important jobs is to connect the dots between day-to-day tasks and the bigger picture.

Start by clearly articulating your organization's values, objectives, vision, and mission. But don't just stick them on a wall and forget about them. Bring them to life in your daily interactions. Share stories of how your work impacts customers or the community. Celebrate moments when your team embodies these values.

Create opportunities for your team to contribute to the larger vision. Maybe it's through brainstorming sessions, cross-functional projects, or volunteer initiatives. When people feel involved in the direction of the organization, their engagement skyrockets.

Now, let's tackle belonging. Humans are social creatures, and we crave connection. Foster a sense of community within your team. This could be through regular team-building activities, mentorship programs, or even just creating space for casual conversations.

One technique I've found effective is the "personal share" at the start of meetings. For a few minutes, everyone should share something from their personal lives—a weekend highlight, a challenge they're facing, or a goal they're working towards.

This humanizes the workplace and builds empathy among team members.

Don't leave yourself out of the equation. As a leader, it's easy to feel isolated. Make an effort to build relationships with other leaders in your organization or industry. Join a leadership group or find a mentor. Having a support network is crucial for your own sense of belonging and motivation.

Promoting Work-Life Balance

Now, let's talk about a topic that's close to my heart: work-life balance. In our always-on, hyper-connected world, it's more important than ever to set boundaries and take care of ourselves.

As a leader, you set the tone for your team. If you constantly send emails at midnight or work through weekends, you're sending a message that this is expected behavior. Instead, model healthy work habits. Take your vacation days. Leave the office at a reasonable hour. Talk openly about your hobbies and interests outside of work.

Encourage your team to do the same. Implement policies that support work-life balance, like flexible working hours or remote work options. But remember, policies are just words on paper if the culture doesn't support them. Actively encourage people to use these benefits without fear of judgment.

One technique I've found helpful is the "energy audit." Track your energy levels throughout the day for a week. When do you feel most focused and productive? When do you start to drag? Use this information to structure your workday around your natural rhythms. Maybe you do your most challenging work in the morning and save administrative tasks for the afternoon slump.

Don't forget about the power of breaks! Encourage your team to step away from their desks regularly. Maybe it's a quick walk around the block or a five-minute meditation session. These small rests can do wonders for productivity and overall well-being.

Practical Advice for Long-Term Motivation

Now, let's get into some nitty-gritty advice for keeping yourself and your team motivated for the long haul.

First up: goal setting. We all know the importance of setting goals, but balancing ambitions and achievability is the key. I like to use the SMART framework (Specific, Measurable, Achievable, Relevant, Time-bound) for setting goals, but with a twist. For each goal, I also identify the "why" behind it. How does this goal connect to our larger mission or personal growth? This connection to purpose can be a powerful motivator when the going gets tough.

Next, let's discuss learning and growth. The moment we stop learning, we start to stagnate. Encourage a culture of continuous learning within your team. This could be through formal training programs, cross-functional projects, or simply setting time aside for reading and reflection.

Consider setting a personal learning goal each quarter. Maybe it's mastering a new skill, reading a challenging book, or attending a conference in a different field. Stepping outside your comfort zone can reignite your passion and bring fresh perspectives to your leadership.

Another powerful tool is the power of storytelling. Humans are wired for narrative. Use stories to illustrate your points, celebrate successes, and learn from failures. Encourage your team to share their stories and create an environment that allows them to share without shame or judgment. This not only builds connection but also helps reinforce key lessons and values.

Let's not forget about the importance of feedback. Create regular opportunities for two-way feedback with your team. This could be through formal reviews or casual check-ins. The key is to make feedback a normal, non-threatening part of your culture. And remember, as a leader, you should actively seek feedback on your own performance, too.

One technique I've found helpful is the "start, stop, continue" framework. Regularly ask your team (and yourself) what you should start, stop, and continue doing. This simple exercise can yield powerful insights and keep you on a path of continuous improvement.

Now, let's talk about resilience. Leadership is demanding, and there will be setbacks along the way, but a resilient nature is the trump card. Building resilience is crucial for long-term success. One way to do this is by reframing challenges as opportunities for growth. When faced with a setback, ask yourself: "What can I learn from this? How can this make me a better leader?"

Another resilience-building technique is the practice of gratitude. Take a few minutes each day to reflect on your gratitude. This could be in a journal or simply a mental exercise. Focusing on the positive can help put challenges in perspective and boost your overall mood and motivation.

Let's not forget about the power of connection. Building and maintaining relationships is crucial for long-term motivation. Make time for one-on-one conversations with your team members. Get to know them as people, not just employees. Understanding their motivations, challenges, and aspirations can help you lead more effectively and create a more engaged team.

For your own motivation, consider finding an accountability partner. This could be a fellow leader, a mentor, or even a friend. Share your goals with them and check in regularly. Having someone to celebrate your wins and support you through challenges can be incredibly motivating.

Finally, remember the importance of celebration. Too often, we achieve a goal and immediately move on to the next challenge without acknowledging our success. Make celebration a regular part of your team culture. This doesn't have to be elaborate – maybe it's a team lunch, a fun activity, or simply taking a moment in a meeting to recognize achievements. Celebrating milestones, both big and small, can help maintain momentum and motivation.

As I wrap up this chapter and this book, I want to leave you with one final thought. Leadership is a journey, not a destination. There will be highs and lows, successes and setbacks. The key is to stay curious, stay connected, and remain committed to your growth and the growth of those around you.

Remember, your motivation as a leader impact more than just you—it ripples out to your team, your organization, and beyond. By implementing these strategies and staying true to your purpose, you can sustain that motivation and engagement for the long run.

So, as you close this book and step back into your leadership role, I challenge you to pick one strategy we've discussed and commit to practicing it this week. Start small, be consistent, and watch as your motivation and engagement flourish. You've got this, leader. Now, go out there and make a difference!

www.ingramcontent.com/pod-product-compliance
Lightning Source LLC
LaVergne TN
LVHW090407210926
848480LV00002B/479
9798330417360